CUCKOO'S NEST

CHRIS CHORLTON

CUCKOO'S NEST

Reminiscences, Reflections, and Ramblings of a Life—So Far

A Mississauga Lakeshore Rotary Club Project
All royalties to benefit The Rotary Foundation

iUniverse, Inc.
Bloomington

Cuckoo's Nest
Reminiscences, Reflections, and Ramblings of a Life—So Far

iUniverse books may be ordered through booksellers or by contacting:

iUniverse
1663 Liberty Drive
Bloomington, IN 47403
www.iuniverse.com
1-800-Authors (1-800-288-4677)

ISBN: 978-1-4620-1625-9 (sc)
ISBN: 978-1-4620-1626-6 (ebk)

Printed in the United States of America

iUniverse rev. date: 03/20/2012

CONTENTS

Foreword by Wilfrid (Wilf) Wilkinson.. ix

Preface.. xi

Acknowledgements..xv

1.   Bringing Home the Bacon.. 1
2.   The Day My Team Died 5
3.   The Duke of Wellington and Me 9
4.   Sandiway House... 17
5.   The Hypnotist.. 22
6.   A Good Decision 27
7.   Help!.. 32
8.   "You'll Never Meet Anyone in a Bar"... 36
9.   The Dancing Lessons 43
10. A Honeymoon, a Disaster, and a Tragedy 47
11. Grattan's Catch.. 52
12. A Golf Compliment 56
13. Going on Vacation 61
14. Moving the Piano 63
15. My Treatment of Doctors 68
16. Anne Chorlton 71
17. Good Old D16 78
18. Playing Happy Families, Relatively Speaking..................................... 81
19. Reorganization: Don't Let It Get You Down....................................... 88
20. The Best Caesar Salad 91
21. The Cost of a Haircut 95
22. Have Another Cookie, Mr. Strong... 98
23. A Humerus Story 102
24. Cats in My Life 108

25. Last Day at the Office 112
26. Goodbye to a Friend 116
27. A Handyman's Comeuppance 120
28. Updating the Will 123
29. Outfoxing the Squirrels 126
30. Liam's First Christmas 131
31. The Man in Tim Hortons 135
32. The Cataract Operation 138
33. The One of a Kind Show 141
34. An Invitation to Dinner 145
35. Rotary and the Khethokuhle Child Care Centre........ 149
36. God Bless Tom 155
37. Selling the Fridge.. 159
38. Coping with my Stutter... 164
39. Taking Pictures... 167

Resources 173

For Ena

FOREWORD BY WILFRID (WILF) WILKINSON

I enjoy talking about Rotary and the work of The Rotary Foundation to clubs that I visit or individuals that I meet.

Some months ago, I was contacted by Chris Chorlton, a member of the Mississauga Lakeshore Rotary Club. We chatted about the local and international projects The Rotary Foundation undertakes. He was particularly interested in the Global Polio Eradication Initiative being carried out with our partners: The World Health Organization; UNICEF; The Center for Disease Control; and more recently, the Bill and Melinda Gates Foundation—not to mention the governments of more than 200 countries, including the more than 120 that have become polio-free since Rotary created this largest public/private health-care campaign in the history of the world.

Rotarian Chris told me that for some years he had been writing short stories about his personal experiences and the people he had met. He was planning to publish these stories and wondered if, with the support of his own club, he could help The Rotary Foundation by donating to it any royalties from the sale of the book. The funds raised would be used by the Foundation to continue its good work, not only for polio eradication but for humanitarian projects all over the world.

He asked if I would consider writing a foreword for his book. He sent me a final draft of *Cuckoo's Nest* that I could review to help me decide, and he asked for my honest opinion on the interest of his stories to others. This was an offer that I couldn't refuse, because one of my key duties as a trustee is to raise money for the Foundation. I accepted gladly.

Much to my surprise and great pleasure, I found that I could relate very quickly to the stories, which were all told with a dash of humour, a touch of sadness, a pinch of whimsy, and a little dose of reality. *Cuckoo's Nest* brings people in everyday events and situations to life, with some surprises. I couldn't help reflecting on some similar experiences of my own. I was pleased to tell Chris that I would be delighted to write this foreword.

Everyone will have their own favourite story. I particularly enjoyed the story about him and his wife being invited formally to their son's home for dinner and the ensuing anticipation of, speculation about, and possible reaction to an announcement that they were not sure would materialize. There is also a story of driving a male friend to the hospital and being mistaken for his same-sex partner, which provided much food for thought. There are many more.

I know you will enjoy reading *Cuckoo's Nest*. And by buying it you will be helping The Rotary Foundation continue its humanitarian work around the world.

Wilf Wilkinson, C.M.
President, Rotary International 2007–08
Chair, The Rotary Foundation 2012–13
Trenton, Ontario
December 2011

PREFACE

I have always looked for opportunities to develop my interest in writing, particularly those where I could have some fun with words—even in serious work or family situations.

Like many people, I longed to write a novel, and consistent with the belief that you should write about what you know, I gathered material about the electricity industry, in which I have had the good fortune to work for nearly 40 years, on both sides of the Atlantic. But I had always been able to put off my efforts to start the actual writing because of the pressures of work and family life.

I had no further excuse when I took early retirement in December 2000—I now had the opportunity to write my novel. I started with a great plot but didn't get very far; I was having trouble developing my characters. I was reluctant to invest the time to write 300 pages before I could confirm a bad result, so I gave up—perhaps only temporarily—on fiction.

I looked around for other vehicles to satisfy my writing urge and found non-fiction short stories. I had no trouble thinking of topics: things that had happened to me at work or at home; things that occurred to me as I going about my daily business; things that I had tucked away, thinking, *That would make an interesting story.* I scribbled down some initial topics, which quickly became an inventory that I continue to add to, and I began to carry a notebook around with me. From this inventory I wrote my first batch of six stories, all of which are in this book. It took me far longer to complete them than I had ever imagined it would! I showed them timidly to my family, who liked them, and they gave me the encouragement I needed to continue.

I sent a few to *The Toronto Star*, and many months later, I was thrilled to hear from Kevin Maclean that they wanted to publish "Last Day at the Office." I wrote in fits and starts. After all, I wasn't on a deadline; I was writing for my own enjoyment, and I didn't have a particular product in mind. For months on end I wouldn't write, and then a particular subject would grab my attention for a few days. A couple of years ago, I also received considerable encouragement from John Stewart, of *The Mississauga News*, which published "God Bless Tom." This was a story I had written immediately after a moving Remembrance Day ceremony I'd attended. And quite recently, three more stories, "Outfoxing the Squirrels," "Coping with my Stutter," and "A Handyman's Comeuppance" were published in *The Globe and Mail*, thanks to Lori Fazari.

At first, my audience was my family and friends, particularly my four grandsons, who I hope will live to almost the end of this century. Their families will be able to read about events that happened to their ancestors up to 150 years before, and that gives me pleasure today.

It has taken me nine years to complete *Cuckoo's Nest*. I might have had the idea somewhere in my mind that someday the stories would be put into a book, but it was not top of mind, at least not of *my* mind. Then, some months ago, my wife, Ena, said, "It's time." Backing her words with action—which is one of her many strengths—she bought a self-publishing package with iUniverse, which galvanized me into completing some unfinished stories and embarking on the seemingly endless editing that is required.

One problem I had was deciding on the sequence of the stories. Generally, I have placed them in a rough chronological sequence, reflecting the time period they cover rather than when they were written, with a couple of exceptions.

I am grateful for all those who are the subjects of my stories, and wherever practical, I have obtained their permission to publish. Mostly I have used real names, except where it was not appropriate, in my judgment, to do so. If anyone is in any way offended by what I have written, I am sorry, for that was never my intent. I should also clarify that *Cuckoo's Nest*, while autobiographical, is not an autobiography per se. Consequently, there are some friends or family members who have been, and are, important in my life but who are not mentioned in *Cuckoo's Nest*.

I also had a problem in coming up with a title. Ena was again a source of inspiration in suggesting *Cuckoo's Nest*, but I should explain where that title came from. Liam, my oldest grandson, was about one year old when he began speaking his first words. For reasons unbeknownst to us, and of course to him, he started calling me using the sound *cuckoo*. At that age, of course, it was just a sound, and he would not have known a cuckoo from a robin, but that name has stuck, and that's what he and his family call me still—producing some slightly embarrassing, but highly amusing, situations when the name is used in public.

Through Rotary, Ena and I have derived great satisfaction from our contributions to the community over the years, the friendships we have made, and the fellowship we have enjoyed. As a result, we have decided that any royalties arising from this book will go to The Rotary Foundation to help them with their wonderful work around the world in alleviating hunger, thirst, disease, and illiteracy. I am grateful for the endorsement and support of the Mississauga Lakeshore Rotary Club, my own club, in promoting *Cuckoo's Nest* and to Wilfrid (Wilf) Wilkinson, President of Rotary International 2007–08 and Chair of The Rotary Foundation 2012–13, for writing the foreword.

Any objectives I might have had have already been met by writing the stories. Anything more is a bonus. I have grown attached to my stories, partly because of the memories and associations they bring back to me and partly because of the pleasure they have given me in writing them. It is my sincere hope that others will enjoy reflecting on their similar experiences while reading about mine.

Chris Chorlton

Mississauga
December 2011

ACKNOWLEDGEMENTS

Thanks to my children, Lisa and Martin, and their spouses, Mark and Janice, respectively, for the encouragement they have given me in writing my stories; for permission to publish some personal details of their lives; and for the special joy and pleasure that their children, Liam, Luke, Damon, and Tyler, bring to Ena and me.

Thanks to other family members and friends who are the subjects of my stories.

Thanks to iUniverse for their expert help in publishing *Cuckoo's Nest*.

Thanks to Wilfrid Wilkinson, President of Rotary International 2007–08 and Chair of The Rotary Foundation 2012–13, for writing the foreword and for his enthusiastic support.

Thanks to Rotary District Governor Brian Carmichael and Past District Governor Bernd Dinnert for their advice and guidance.

Thanks to the Board of Directors, particularly President Liz Durdan and Past President Bruce Brown, and all members of the Mississauga Lakeshore Rotary Club for their encouragement and support. Thanks to the treasurer, Peter Newhouse, CA, for agreeing to audit the royalties received and the donations made to The Rotary Foundation.

Thanks to Kevin MacLean, of *The Toronto Star*; John Stewart, of *The Mississauga News*; and Lori Fazari, of *The Globe and Mail,* for their encouragement in publishing some of my stories.

Thanks to *The Times* for extracts from their edition of June 22, 1815.

Thanks to the copyright holders for the brief extracts from the lyrics of the John Lennon/Paul McCartney songs "She Loves You," "Ticket to Ride," and "Hey Jude."

Thanks to Torstar Syndication Services for permission to reprint the illustration associated with "Last Day at the Office."

Thanks to David Martindale for providing advice and some photographs associated with the story on the Khethokuhle Child Care Centre.

Thanks to the charity Soul of Africa for the use of material from their website.

Thanks to Toby Gardiner, of RJ Entertainment Publishing, who provided the photograph of Tom Jackson associated with "God Bless Tom."

Thanks to Ben Clarkson for permission to use his illustration associated with "Coping with My Stutter."

Finally, heartfelt thanks to my wife, Ena, who encouraged me to write, contributed ideas and suggestions, proofread the text, provided computer help when needed, and took practical steps to bring *Cuckoo's Nest* to fruition. Without Ena there would be no book.

1

BRINGING HOME THE BACON

During the Second World War, and for a few years after, my father looked for ways to help supplement the rations of the time. Fortunately, we lived in a rambling house built around the turn of the century, with spacious gardens. The front garden was formal, and so it was at the back that we played our games. There we had gooseberry and blackberry bushes and a variety of fruit trees: apple, pear, and damson. The berries were collected when ripe and made into jams or pies. The other fruit was collected in the fall and either made into sauce and bottled or laid carefully on shelves lined with newspaper in the cool cellar. All these efforts were successful and enriched our lives and our table for years. My father then grew more ambitious and decided to try raising hens.

We acquired several hens, the breed of which I have long since forgotten. The eggs were good, but we were troubled by foxes, and we didn't have the hens more than a year or two before the henhouse was struck by lightning and burned to the ground.

The next venture was mushrooms. My father read an article about how easy it was to grow them at home. He bought several bales of straw, which were deposited in our cellar. I helped him water the straw and turn it occasionally, so it would generate heat. When the straw reached the right temperature, we planted the mushroom spores. This venture was a complete failure. All that came out was about a pound and a half of mouldy mushrooms. My mother threw them out, closely followed by the straw—but my father was allowed to stay.

Undaunted, my father had his next brilliant idea. We all loved bacon and pork so, his logic went, why not raise a pig ourselves and eliminate the middleman—in this case, our local pork butcher, who also happened to be a member of my father's Rotary club. Soon afterwards, a man came to build the pig sty. The word "sty" has an unpleasant sound to it. But this sty was different. Strong new timbers were used to build the sleeping quarters, with a sloping roof and a door that led out to the outdoor yard. Entrance to the sty was through a big gate with a latch, a padlock, and strong hinges. The roof was covered with roofing material to keep the rain out, and any gaps between the beams were plugged. Finally, the sty was painted in creosote, then in common use but forbidden today, to preserve the wood for generations of pigs to come. It all looked very snug.

My father knew a number of farmers, and from one of them, probably another Rotarian, he bought a piglet. It was little and pink with a curly tail. I don't remember whether it was male or female, but Christine, my sister, Graham, my brother, and I decided to call it Snowball.

Snowball changed our daily rituals. All vegetable peelings and wastes were now collected, and once or twice a week were put, along with some meal, into a very large saucepan and boiled for hours. The result was a porridge-like concoction, the smell of which permeated the whole house. It looked very unappetizing to us, but Snowball found it very tasty.

Snowball became the focus of our attentions. After school we would rush to see her (I am assuming with a name like Snowball it was probably female). We fed her. We sat on the sides of the sty with our legs dangling inside. Snowball didn't seem to mind. She listened while we told her stories. Snowball was a very undemanding part of the family, and you could always rely on her to be in the same place. We played our games around the sty. The roof of the sty was a popular spot, because from there you could sit and survey the surrounding garden or you could climb higher on the apple tree, whose branches overhung the sty.

The days and weeks passed. Snowball grew, as I suppose we all did. As she got bigger, she grunted more and scratched herself against the wooden sides of the sty. Now we kept our legs outside the sty, because she looked and acted as though she wouldn't stand any nonsense. But she was still Snowball to us. Once a week my father would don his Wellington boots and clean out the sty. The old straw would go on a pile where it would mature and later be put on the roses, and it would be replaced by fresh, sweet-smelling straw.

I don't know how long it takes for a pig to grow to full size, but eventually the day came when my father told us that Snowball would be going away soon, and that "people" would come to collect her. While we had known from the beginning that Snowball would move on sometime, I realize now that we did not fully understand when and to where.

I remember the morning quite clearly when my mother told us that we were going to have a surprise outing that day, and the three of us were bundled into the car. We were about to drive down the driveway, when a big van pulled in, blocking our way. These were the "people" who had come to collect Snowball. The vehicles shifted around so we could proceed. As we were leaving, we began to hear squeals. The squeals came from Snowball, and they went on for what seemed to us an eternity before the car moved out of range. I can still hear those squeals now.

A few days later, the same van came to our house. The next thing I remember is being taken to the cellar, where we were shown two sides of an animal hanging on hooks. This was Snowball, who was ready to be cured. This involved rubbing salt into the flesh, but to us it was like rubbing salt into raw wounds. We all participated in this, and our parents sought to encourage us by telling us that there would be sufficient pork to feed us for months. This was bad enough, but worse was to come.

Some time later, when we sat down to breakfast one morning, my mother presented us with plates containing bacon, fried eggs, and tomatoes, my favourite breakfast. I looked down, picked up the fork, and moved the bacon around on the plate. After a minute, I put down my fork and declared, "I can't eat Snowball." One by one the rest of the family did the same, even my parents. None of us could eat Snowball. We gave away what was left of Snowball to grateful neighbours and friends.

We didn't have another pig. The sty was cleared of straw and became a full-time play house, the envy of our friends. But I never forgot Snowball. And I understood from then on why farmers never name their animals.

The would-be, tried-to-be, and failed-to-be
successful pig-farming Chorlton family

Arthur and Anne with Graham, me, and Christine, smiling enough for all
us children, around 1948

2

THE DAY MY TEAM DIED

I knew something was wrong. My mother was looking out of the front-room window, waiting for me, as I walked down the drive coming home from school. As I approached the door, I wondered what could have happened. Was someone ill? Or had someone died? Nothing could have prepared me for the news Mum was about to impart. She opened the door, her face pale, and blurted, "There's been a plane crash. The United plane . . ." Her voice trailed off, and she didn't finish the sentence; she couldn't finish the sentence. She didn't have to clarify to me what "United" she was talking about.

For as long as I could remember, "United" had meant only one thing: Manchester United. My father had been born in Manchester and had been a season-ticket holder in the late '20s and the '30s. He had brought me up on stories of United. To be truthful, since the team had mixed success at best in that era, most of the stories were not that complimentary and involved relegation struggles and lurching from one crisis to another. From Dad I learned about Joe Spence, Tommy Manley, and "gentleman" Lal Hilditch, who happened to live near us in Northwich. Dad also told me about his offer of money to United for a campaign to recruit the legendary Stanley Matthews in the late '30s. The cumulative effect of all this on me was to cultivate a loyalty and a passion for the club, which remains to this day.

In those days, we couldn't travel the seventeen miles to Manchester often. Most Saturdays Dad and I watched Northwich Victoria in the Cheshire League. Our eyes and bodies might have been there, but our hearts and minds were with United, and it was United we followed. Every Saturday evening I rushed to the newsagent for the Saturday evening pink paper for the full results and report. Mum always told everyone that a

United loss spoiled the weekend for us all. Fortunately, from the time I was aware of supporting them, when I was about eight, they didn't lose often. Some of my friends were also United supporters, but I was different from them. After all, United was part of my heritage; they had merely climbed on the United bandwagon later.

Pronouncements by United's Manager, Matt Busby, were gospel in our house. I read everything I could about United and the "Busby babes": the cultured Roger Byrne; cheeky Eddie Coleman, with the swivelling hips; the rapier-like Dennis Viollet; the artistic Irishman, Liam Whelan; and Tommy Taylor, the perfect centre-forward. But most of all, there was Duncan Edwards. Capped by England at 18, Duncan at 21 was a colossus, as strong as an ox but fair and blessed with incredible stamina and a powerful shot with either foot. More than 50 years have gone by, but I still can recall in my mind this picture of Duncan . . . "he wins the ball with a crunching tackle in mid-field [it should be called mud-field, because the grounds in those days always seemed to be muddy, and that is how the ground is in my picture], shrugs off challenges from several defenders, advances towards the penalty area, and unleashes a terrific shot which, never rising more than a foot, explodes in the net." Duncan was my idol.

In early February 1958, United visited the mighty Arsenal, and I remember the expectation surrounding the game. With the nervous anticipation known to all sport followers, I tuned the radio at five o'clock to hear the football scores. The announcer soon came to the result I had been waiting for: "Arsenal 4" he intoned—my heart dropped in the face of a likely defeat—"Manchester United," his voice rising, "5!" They had won and Duncan Edwards had scored the first goal! Shortly after that, the team left for an important European Cup tie in Belgrade the following Wednesday, which they drew 3-3 and progressed to the next round on aggregate. On the way home on February 6, the United plane stopped to refuel at Munich and crashed after attempting to take off from a slushy runway.

"Is it bad?" was all I could say to my mother, who put her arm round me as we went to the kitchen where there was a report on the radio. Yes, it was bad, almost as bad as it could possibly be. The early reports talked of death and serious casualties, and we sat as a family grieving together, glued to the radio and television.

Later that night, I took my portable radio, usually used for listening to Jack Jackson and others on Radio Luxembourg, to bed with me. With it tucked beneath the blankets so as not wake Graham, my younger brother, sleeping in the next bed, I listened for the names of victims and survivors. I prayed for them all but Duncan in particular. I found myself trying to make deals with God in the hope that Duncan would survive. I even offered a macabre trade—take some of the others, but spare Duncan. At some point there was a roll call on the radio. With the aid of a flashlight, I ticked off the names as they were announced: Byrne, Taylor, Pegg, Colman, Whelan—the cumulative loss of those who had died immediately was overwhelming. The list went on and on. There were 23 deaths in all, including players, club officials, journalists, and some private individuals. *But what about Duncan Edwards?* When at last I heard Duncan was amongst the survivors, the tears started to flow, and I cried myself to sleep.

The next few days were a blur, as the enormity of what had happened sank in to all. Initially the news of Duncan was encouraging, but it soon became clear that his injuries were severe and would have already killed a lesser man. Somehow, this time allowed me to come to terms with the possibility of his passing, and two weeks later he succumbed to his injuries and died. Football had lost one of its greats, and I had lost my idol.

By then, steps had been taken for the club to begin life anew. Eleven days after the crash, with a team made up of newly signed players, promoted reserves, and two survivors, United miraculously defeated Sheffield Wednesday in the FA Cup. They then went on to win in the next round in a replay against West Bromwich Albion, with Bobby Charlton, playing his second game since the crash, dashing along the wing in the last minute to cross for the winning goal. Public sentiment for United became very emotional, and much of the attention was focused on Bobby. He had been a very talented player before the crash but was now playing as if inspired. Only 20, he was quick, with a good body swerve and a terrific shot. Gradually he began to fill the space in this 14-year-old schoolboy's heart for a football hero. United reached the final at Wembley, which I attended without my father—who had become ill and would never see United again. They lost, but the result could not extinguish the rise of the United phoenix, epitomized for me by Bobby Charlton.

Now, 50 years on, I live in Canada and fortunately can watch most United games live on television. Even the glories of United's success over the last 20 years cannot eclipse my memories. All I have to do is shut my eyes, and I am back at a blustery, overcast Old Trafford on a midwinter afternoon, with the wind in my face and United playing toward the Stretford end in the second half. *In midfield, Duncan Edwards wins the ball with a crunching tackle, shrugs off a couple of defenders, and advances into the penalty area and . . .*

As if it were yesterday.

The Munich memorial at Manchester United's Old Trafford stadium—"The Theatre of Dreams." Duncan Edwards is the first player on the left in the team picture taken before the game in Belgrade.

3

THE DUKE OF WELLINGTON AND ME

Nothing except a battle lost can be half as melancholy as a
battle won.
—Duke of Wellington, dispatch from Waterloo, 1815

I love history. Growing up in England may have helped because history is all around you there. My school, the King's School, Chester, was founded by Henry VIII in 1542 after the dissolution of the monasteries. For a few years I attended the school in premises adjacent to the cathedral before it moved to more salubrious surroundings on the outskirts of the city. The new school was opened in 1962 by a descendant, by marriage, of King Hal's—Queen Elizabeth, The Queen Mother. Perhaps as a result, studying the Tudors always seemed more relevant to me than if I had attended a school founded in more modern times. To me, the intricacies of court intrigue and Henry's attempts to ensure male lineage for his throne were fascinating and easy to understand—I didn't need the famous doggerel for remembering the fates of Henry's six wives: divorced, beheaded, died, beheaded, divorced, survived!

The opening of the new school by the Queen Mother was a memorable occasion, and preparations for her visit were extensive. The climax of the formal opening was her speech in the school hall in front of the pupils of the school (then all boys but now co-ed) and associated dignitaries. I remember two things quite vividly. Her speech included the word *patina* and she enunciated precisely its consonants. I had never heard the word *patina* before. I discovered it meant the antique appearance of tarnished metal. Why I should remember that and why it was relevant is one of the mysteries of life. The other highlight was the custom for the head boy at the time—whose name I have forgotten, but in any event I would not want to embarrass him by finding it out and naming him here—to ask the school for a special cheer for Her Majesty. I can see him now, standing up in front of the biggest audience he had ever experienced, after practicing his part many times, no doubt.

"Three cheers for Her Majesty Queen Elizabeth, The Queen Mother!" he exhorted us. "Hip, hip!"

"Hooray!" was the spirited reply.

"Hip, hip!"

"Hooray!" thundered the assembly. And then came the part that must still haunt his dreams. Perhaps he realized he was close to the end of his part in the proceedings and relaxed his guard. He should have gone on to shout the third and final "hip, hip," but—

"Hooray!" he shouted in triumph instead, before realizing his error—which unfortunately couldn't be corrected. We couldn't help laughing, and the Queen Mother looked on quite amused and apparently not at all concerned that she was two "hips" short!

I have a good memory for dates. Now that I am in Canada and have been a Canadian for more than 40 years, I wonder what the most significant key dates might be in Canadian history. The charter for the Hudson Bay Company in 1670? The Plains of Abraham in 1759? The war of 1812? Confederation in 1867 or Vimy Ridge in 1917?

There are a lot of such key dates in British history. Perhaps the most famous date is 1066, the Battle of Hastings, when Duke William from Normandy defeated Harold the Anglo-Saxon king in the first major British/French confrontation and became king of England. There are many other dates that commemorate other British/French battles, from Agincourt in 1415 to Trafalgar in 1805 and Waterloo in 1815. In fact, I have always been surprised that the stretch of water between England and France is called the English Channel. If it hadn't existed, I am sure both countries would have felt the need to create it—a mutual moat, as it were.

The Battle of Waterloo is the link to this story. It took place in 1815, during the Regency period, when George III was deemed not fit to govern and instead his authority was exercised by his son, the Prince Regent, later George IV. George was known for his extravagance, his womanizing, and his patronage of the arts. By then, Jane Austen had published three of her novels, including *Pride and Prejudice* in 1813, and would die two years later, in 1817. Our image of those times has, of course, been conditioned by the many TV and movie productions of her novels over the past 20 years. We know, of course, there while there was genteel living for the wealthy few, there was abject poverty for the many poor. The population of Britain was about 10 million, with high unemployment, industrial unrest (particularly in the cotton mills surrounding Manchester), and concern that the revolution in France would spread across the Channel. But I am getting ahead of myself.

Let me go back to one Saturday in the mid-fifties, when my father asked me to accompany him on what he described as a "duty call." One of his friends at church had told him about an old lady who had moved into a retirement home and who had an old bureau she wanted to sell. Dad's ears must have pricked up on two counts. First, he was always willing to help those in need, and secondly, the word *bureau* piqued his interest.

I remember that we went to a very large old house in Sandiway, not far from where I had been born. The house had been divided into a number of apartments. This lady lived on the second floor, in a lovely unit overlooking the front garden. Dad knocked at the door. The lady came to answer it. Dad must have called ahead of time, because she was expecting him. He quickly introduced himself and me. She ushered us in through the entranceway into her living room, which was small but perfectly adequate for her, except that it was dominated by a very large piece of furniture along one wall. After she had made the customary pot of tea, along with milk (poured in first) and sugar (one teaspoon, added last)—once in Canada I learned to do without milk and sugar— she got straight to business.

"This is the bureau that you have heard about," she said as she stood up by the side of it, which was nearly as tall as she was and a good five feet in length. It was made of solid mahogany and glowed a deep reddish-brown. The base contained a series of drawers, large ones at the bottom and smaller ones above. On top of the base there was a slanted front, with a simple but very elegant rectangular marquetry pattern. It was hinged, and when opened out it rested on elegant sliders and formed the writing surface. She opened the front lid, and we saw several little drawers with vertical wooden dividers at each side, ideal for storing papers and such things. Of course, this is how I remember it now. At the time, being barely a teenager, I wasn't really much interested in it at all, but my father was enthralled by it. It certainly wasn't an ordinary old desk.

"The bureau was in my late husband's family for many years," the woman said, "but as you can see, it's much too big for me to keep now, and I would like it to go to a good home."

"How much would you like for it?" my father asked.

"Would 25 pounds be reasonable?" she asked tentatively. Dad thought for a minute.

"I'm happy to give you 30," he told her. Even then I realized that he thought she hadn't asked enough and he didn't want to take advantage of an old lady. In those days, 30 pounds was quite a sum, equal to about three weeks of the average industrial worker's pay. In addition, of course, Dad had to pay for the moving costs, as it was a large, heavy piece. The lady was delighted, and the deal was struck.

Soon afterwards, the bureau was delivered to our house, which had spacious rooms, but the only place the bureau would fit comfortably was in our large hall. Unfortunately, we couldn't work at it because of the through traffic in the hall, which was disappointing. We used the bureau for storing and filing papers, and over time it became full.

Some years later, I was looking for an envelope containing some photographs that I knew was in the bureau but didn't know exactly where. After I had been through the drawers in the base, I opened the lid and pulled out every drawer in the top. The envelope was not there. I wondered if it had slipped behind the dividers. I had difficulty getting my fingers in; it was so cluttered up that I had to really stretch them. Then I felt something move. I fetched a flashlight so I could see better, and I saw that a slim vertical wooden drawer had partially slid out. I put my fingers in again, got a better grip, and pulled it out. It was obviously a secret compartment—this was not something that you would normally find unless you knew it was there. Stuffed into this compartment were papers. I pulled them out. I realized quickly that they were old newspapers, so I spread them out very carefully on the kitchen table. As I examined them, I became quite excited. These weren't just any old papers.

The first one that caught my attention was a copy *The Times* (cost of six pence), dated June 22, 1815, and just above the paper's banner was handwritten, "Not to be torn. Account of the Battle of Waterloo." I couldn't believe my eyes! For someone as interested in history as I, this was a real find! The paper was very fragile, but as I turned the front page I came across several accounts of the battle and the official bulletin from Downing Street, which is reproduced here.

LONDON TUESDAY, JUNE 22, 1815

OFFICIAL BULLETIN.

"DOWNING STREET, June 22 1815

"The Duke of WELLINGTON's Dispatch, dated, Waterloo, the 19 June, states, that on the preceding day BUONAPARTE attacked, with his whole force, the British line supported by a corps of Prussians; which attack, after a long and sanguinary conflict, terminated in the complete Overthrow of the Enemy's Army, with the loss of ONE HUNDRED & FIFTY pieces of CANNON and TWO EAGLES.

During the night, the Prussians under Marshal BLUCHER, who joined in the pursuit of the enemy, captured SIXTY GUNS, and a large part of BUONAPARTE's BAGGAGE. The allied armies continued to pursue the enemy. Two French Generals were taken.

Such is the great and glorious result of those masterly movements by which the Hero of Britain met and frustrated the audacious attempt of the Rebel Chief, Glory to WELLINGTON, to our gallant Soldiers, and to our brave Allies! BUONAPARTE's reputation has been wrecked and his last grand stake has been lost in this tremendous conflict. TWO HUNDRED AND TEN PIECES OF CANNON captured in a single battle, put to the blush the boasting column of the Place de Vendome. Long and sanguinary, indeed, we fear, the conflict must have been; but the boldness of the Rebel Frenchmen was the boldness of despair and conscience sate heavy on those arms which were raised against their Sovereign, against their

Official Bulletin, *The Times*, June 22, 1815

Naturally, perhaps, my attention was initially drawn to the description of the battle from the various reports and the statements made by Wellington, as well as those from the "Rebel Buonaparte." After a while, my brain became numbed by the detail and flowery language, and I began to look at other parts of the paper. I discovered that Parliament had immediately granted Wellington the sum of 200,000 pounds in gratitude for his victory.

Also reproduced here is an extract from *The Times* that lists some positions vacant for women. Beside these are published the names of some of the wounded officers, with an indication of the extent of their injuries. The contrast between the necessities of domestic life at home and the realities of war in foreign lands was stark.

Lieutenant-Colonel Mackdonell, Coldstream, slightly.

Lieutenant-Colonel Dashwood, 3rd Guards, severely.

Lieutenant-Colonel Sir R. Hill, Royal Horse Guards, Blue severely.

Lieutenant-Colonel Hill.

Lieutenant-Colonel Schrieder, 8th Line Battalion.

Lieutenant-Colonel Adam, 1st Guards, severely.

Lieutenant-Colonel Miller, 1st Guards, dangerously.

Lieutenant-Colonel Sir George Henry Berkeley, A.A.G.

Major Maclean, 73rd.

Major Beckwith, 95th, severely.

Major Jessop, Assistant-Quarter-Master-General.

Major Burche, 1st Light, Bat., K.G.L., right arm amputated.

Major Parkinson, 73rd, severely.

Major Parker, R.H., Artillery leg amputated.

Major Robe, Ball, Royal Artillery, severely.

Major Hamilton, Aide-de-Camp to General Sir E. Barnes.

Major Lindsay, 69th Regiment, severely.

Major Watson, 69th Regiment, severely.

B. M. Emem, dangerously.

L. Wilkin, 95th Regiment, severely.

Major Miller, 95th Regiment, severely.

Captain Smith, 95th Regiment, severely.

Captain Taylor, Aide-de-Camp to Sir Thomas Picton, slightly.

Captain Dance, 23rd Light Dragoons.

Captain Johnson 95th Regiment.

Captain Carments, 95th Regiment.

Captains Darney, Napier, A.M., Donald, Webber, Royal Artillery, severely.

Captain Dumaresque, Aide-de-Camp to General Sir J. Byng, severely.

Captain Whynnater, Royal Artillery, severely.

Captain Barnes, Brigade Major Royal Artillery, severely.

Captain the Hon.——Erskine, D.A.A.G., left arm amputated.

Captain A. Dangten, Aide-de-Camp to Lieutenant-General Picton, severely.

Lieutenant Foster, Royal Artillery, severely.

Lieutenant Crome, Royal Artillery, severely.

Lieutenant Robe, Royal Artillery, severely.

Lieutenant Smith, Royal Artillery, severely.

WANT PLACES—All Letters to be post paid.

AS HOUSEKEEPER, or Cook and Housekeeper, where a Kitchen-maid is kept, a steady person who can have an undeniable character from her last situation. Direct to 5, Little Rider-street, St. James's.

AS HOUSEKEEPER to a single Gentleman, or as upper Servant in a genteel family, or to attend upon two or three young ladies, a middle-aged person who flatters herself, she shall be able to give satisfaction in either capacity. Direct to C. D., at Mr. Williams's, Cheesemonger, 18, Great Winchester-street, Broad-street.

AS LADY'S MAID, or to wait on two young ladies, a young woman who can have an unexceptionable character from her last place where she lived seven years; no objection to go abroad. Direct to G. N., at Miss Kenan's, Dressmaker, 28, Chapel-street, Grosvenor-square.

AS LADY'S MAID, or to wait on two or three young ladies, a respectable young woman; has no objection to take an Upper Housemaid's place; she perfectly understands hair dressing, can work well at her needle, and get up fine linen; can have a good character from the lady she has just left. Direct to C. M., 15, Robert-street, Bedford-row.

AS WET NURSE, a young woman aged 27, first child; has a good breast of milk, and can be well recommended. Direct to E. R., at 21, Paradise-row, Back-road, Islington.

AS WET NURSE, a Person about 22 years of age, without any incumbrance, with a good breast of milk, having lost her first child, and can have a good recommendation; would have no objection to have one at home, but would prefer the former.—Direct, C. W., 2, Mark-street, Paul-street, Shoreditch.

A YOUNG PERSON, aged 23, to attend on one or two young ladies, or as Upper Housemaid in a small family; can work well at her needle, and get up fine linen; no objection to travel.—Direct to J. G., at 251, High Holborn.

A YOUNG WOMAN of Respectable Connections, to attend upon an elderly lady or young ladies. Understands plain dressmaking, getting up fine linen, and can have a good character from the lady she has just left. No objection to travel.—Direct to A. B. 35, Trinity-square.

AS COOK AND HOUSEKEEPER, a Person who perfectly understands her business in both branches, and can have an unexceptionable character from her last place, where she lived two and a-half years.—Direct to A. H., 14, Great Chesterfield-street, Marylebone.

Jobs vacant and wounded officers. Extract
from *The Times*, June 22, 1815

Without much effort, I imagined Mr. Darcy sitting in his study at Pemberley, reading the same paper then as I was now and checking to see if any of his friends, or even the naughty Mr. Wickham, was listed—and perhaps complaining about the trend in commodity prices!

Another of the papers was *The British Volunteer and Manchester Weekly News*, which I subsequently learned was merged in 1825 with the *Manchester Guardian,* the forerunner of today's *Guardian*. This was dated Saturday, June 28, 1815. The actual date of the battle was June 18, but it is unlikely that reports were available for the edition of June 21. Thus, this edition would have been the first of that paper to contain details. In perusing the papers I found a rich store of information about what life was like in those times. A number of tidbits caught my eye:

- "Three stout men, who can bring good character for sobriety, are wanted for the Police Office, Manchester."
- It cost "36 guineas to educate a young gentleman, with full board, per annum."
- "A bottle of oil to destroy bugs" cost two shillings and sixpence.
- "A new coach, The Fox and Grapes, was commencing from Chesterfield to Newark on the 31st Inst."
- "Daniel Davies was left for execution at Stafford for forging a bill of exchange."

Not long ago, I came across an article on Canada from this paper, which is also reproduced here. As you can see, the overall view of Canada at that time is not very complimentary. Most of us would not disagree with the assessment of our climate, and complaints about the cost of living are nothing new, but the comments about the appearance of Canadian women, the state of Canadian art, and aspirations are not very flattering. Let's just say we have come a long way in the past 200 years!

CANADA.

The climate of Canada may in general be considered healthy ; but it is not at first very agreeable to those who arrive from England, or the more southern countries of Europe—it requires a residence of some time to make it pleasant. The winter is too long, and too severe, and the summer is in the other extreme; too short and too warm. The people of Canada make little progress in the useful and elegant arts ; they have little or no ambition, are satisfied if they can live as their forefathers have done, and make no attempt at improvement ; possessed of a sufficiency of land, at a cheap rate, they cultivate little more than what is necessary for their families. The women are subject to a swelling of the neck, the same that has been observed in Switzerland and some of the valleys of the Alps ; it is so common, they seldom attempt the cure of it, and little pains are taken to hide it. Out of twenty young women who expose their necks in a ball-room, fifteen of them will have some appearance of the goitre. When the army arrived in Canada, from being a remarkable cheap country, every article of the first necessity became remarkably dear; in some places not to be had ; there was only sufficient for the inhabitants themselves ; the quantity consumed by the new comers created a scarcity, and but for the Americans, who furnished supplies of fresh beef and flour, the army could not have been supported. The war has been very useful to Canada ; almost every individual has profited by it ; an immense sum of money has been expended in it, and it has excited a desire of acquiring those comforts which wealth commands—a spirit of emulation has begun to appear, which, with the means the war has left behind, will more advance the progress of civilization and the arts in five years, than has been done for the last fifty.

Article on Canada, *British Volunteer and Manchester Weekly News*, July 29, 1815

I have framed pages of the papers that are in the best condition, so they can be read from both sides, and they hang in my office at home. I pass by them several times a day, often stopping to read them. Consequently, I can't help feeling that while the "Iron Duke" and I may not be exactly close friends, we are certainly more than nodding acquaintances. And so, as a mark of respect, three cheers for the Duke of Wellington! Hip, hip . . .

4

SANDIWAY HOUSE

During my nearly 40-year career, I have worked in about 20 different locations on both sides of the Atlantic and probably three times that number of different offices—some in towns but most in cities. What is the best working location I experienced? Let me tell you about Sandiway House, where I first started work.

Sandiway House was a very large, rambling sandstone country house that accommodated about 100 staff as one of four area headquarters of the Merseyside and North Wales Electricity Board, affectionately known then and now as MANWEB. Then it was nationalized, but now it has been privatized. Sandiway House was only about three miles from my home, a comfortable and pleasant walk on a summer's day, especially in the morning, because we didn't start work till 8:50. But, the English climate being what it is, it required a drive most of the time. I was no stranger to Sandiway House. My father had worked there for nearly 20 years before he retired, and I'd attended the annual children's Christmas party and other family social events. More recently I had been a summer student there.

A wealthy businessman built Sandiway House in the 1880s, and it was converted into offices in the 1920s. Sandiway House was hidden from the main Chester Road. The driveway wound round rhododendron bushes and tall beech and horse-chestnut trees before arriving at the imposing front entrance to the house, which was slightly raised up from the surrounding countryside and offered a splendid view of the Cheshire Plain. Once inside, you were in a large hall with a graciously curved staircase to the right. The ground floor accommodated the typing pool, some offices, the senior dining room—admission to which was highly prized—the kitchen, and the dining room for the rest of the staff. To the right of the house, in what were once stables, were the printing shop and stores. Surrounding the house were several acres of beautiful grounds with extensive shrubbery, sweeping perennial borders, beds of roses, and an expansive lawn. Also on the estate, situated further from the house, was the gardener's cottage.

The second floor was for the more senior officers, including the area manager and their support staff. It was there that I began as a graduate trainee on January 1, 1964, working in an office with four others. The two senior staff members were Cliff, a likeable man who managed the salaries and wages of the company, including the various union agreements, which he knew inside out; and Arthur, a rather sad looking but very sincere man who was the education and welfare officer.

Cliff had been in the navy, and whenever he referred to his experiences, one of us would say, "Come in number six; your time's up," as though his wartime service had been spent supervising paddleboats at a municipal park, and we would all laugh as heartily as the first time we had heard it.

Arthur was more serious and had been in the army throughout the war but, much to his annoyance, never got closer to the front than Aldershot. He had some old-fashioned views and thought that married women shouldn't be earning "pin money, taking jobs from male breadwinners."

Assisting Cliff was Harry, a tall, slim man, very street smart, with a gift for the gab, and usually the instigator of any prank in our office. John, who happened to be going out with the daughter of our next-door neighbour, assisted Arthur. As a trainee, my job was to learn the business, pitch in to help where needed, and carry out special projects.

Our office wasn't a large room, and we shared two phones between the five of us. The others all smoked, so there was a haze most of the time, although it didn't really bother me. With five people in such a small space, it was critical that we got on well, and fortunately we did.

Our work dress was quite formal. Most days I wore a suit with a white shirt and tie. The jacket might come off on a warm summer's day but would be quickly put back on if we were summoned across the hallway to the spacious office of our boss. This was Peter Henderson, the area secretary, who had been a prisoner of war in Japan for several years. Paradoxically, he became particularly interested in all things Japanese, and I thought perhaps it was his way of coping with his ordeal.

Some days would be very busy, particularly at the end of a month, or a year, when reports had to be filed. Today, of course, they would all be prepared on and by computer. At that time, we had to have the reports, with any calculations laboriously checked on an adding machine, typed onto stencils that we proofread by reading them out to each other, before they were printed on the Gestetner machines in the printing shop. This was run by Stan Gregory, a soft-hearted man with a deep voice, who had been in the navy. Most of the senior staff had served in some capacity during the war.

At other times the pace was more leisurely, and as we worked we could discuss a topical issue or end up having some fun—which usually involved Harry. Once he told us about a racing columnist who was attracting a following by each day recommending a horse to win, usually a heavy favourite. Any winnings were reinvested the next day on another horse he would pick. We first became interested when the winning streak reached five. We thought, *Why not?* We put a pound each into the kitty. At lunchtime Harry went to the local bookie's to place the five-pound bet—Harry being the only one of us who had ever placed a bet or knew where to go. The race was at three o'clock, and just before then, Harry pulled out a radio and we listened to the race, hoping, of course, that we would not be interrupted by work. The race was exciting because of our bet, and the horse won at three to two on. We had made a profit of three pounds, six shillings and eightpence between us— not much perhaps, but we were hooked.

The next day Harry placed the bet on the horse recommended by the racing guru. Again our horse won, this time at better odds of two to one, as we huddled close to the radio, like French resistance fighters listening to coded radio messages on the BBC. Now we were on a roll, and our stake had risen to about 25 pounds. We were ecstatic, although we had to control ourselves in front of other staff. And, of course, to this point the winnings were small. But for a few days it dominated our office, and we giggled whenever something happened that reminded us of the name of the horse that day. We discussed whether to pay out some of our winnings as a dividend but decided to continue. Our luck held for another couple of days and then our horse lost. We all agreed to stop there, before it got out of hand, but it was great fun while it lasted.

The gardens were maintained by Mr. Stubbs and two labourers. Mr. Stubbs lived in a small cottage on the estate; the head gardener, he was a stern man most of the time but could occasionally be persuaded to laugh with a deep guffaw. The gardeners grew fruit and vegetables for the canteen and also washed the cars of the senior staff. Surplus produce was sold to the staff, and during the summer I would regularly go home laden with lettuce, cabbage, radishes, and Cheshire potatoes.

Mrs. Adamson, the head cook, ruled the kitchen and her two assistant cooks. No one dared to confront Mrs. Adamson, and Arthur, to whom she reported, quaked at the prospect of giving her direction on some matter or other. Sometimes, passing the kitchen, we heard raised voices—Mrs. Adamson's always being the loudest—and occasionally even crying from Vera, the junior assistant. Mrs. Adamson, it has to be said, was a terrific cook. Although generally scrupulous with her standards of cleanliness in the kitchen—for example, the kitchen staff wore hairnets—she would incongruously stand over the stove with a cigarette in her mouth. Nevertheless, the meals were always tasty and wholesome, and heaven help anyone who left food on the plate; she took it as a personal insult. Deep down she had a sensitive side, and if someone had special dietary needs because they were recuperating from an illness, she took great care in catering to them.

After lunch in the summer we played bowls on the lawn, competing for a prestigious trophy. The lawn was overlooked by the senior dining room, and I am sure that not a few careers were influenced by the demeanour, and the prowess, displayed on the bowling green. As we played, we sometimes saw glimpses, as I assume the senior staff did, of Susan and Robert wandering around the grounds hand in hand. Susan and Robert were the closest we came at Sandiway House to a scandal. Susan was attractive, bright, and single; she was the secretary assigned to our office. Robert was ten or more years older, a well-known local cricketer, liked by all, and a very eligible suitor for Susan in every respect but one—and in those days a very important one. He was already married. Their courtship was a public secret. Sometimes when Susan was in our office to take dictation, Cliff would offer some fatherly words of advice to her; these were always taken in the spirit in which they were offered but never followed.

We were a close-knit community at Sandiway House. We celebrated marriages and births. We mourned deaths. We helped those that needed help. Everyone knew everyone else, and everyone's role was respected and appreciated. A number of social and sporting events were held throughout the year, which fostered this spirit. Car rallies, picnics, and treasure hunts were held in the summer and theatre outings and a Christmas dance in the winter.

I attended two of the Christmas dances while I was there. I didn't have a regular girlfriend, and the first time I took Harry's sister, who I had never met before. The second time I was in a quandary who I could ask. Unbeknownst to me, my problem had been detected. One day I received a small deputation from the typing pool with a suggestion. They told me that their colleague, June, did not have a partner for the dance either, and that if I were to ask June she would be glad to come with me. June was a pleasant girl, a few years older than me, and I knew her father, who belonged to the same cricket club as I did. It was a good solution, or so it seemed. However, I likely took June's acceptance too much for granted, because when I asked her, fairly casually as we passed in the corridor, if she would come to the dance with me, much to my surprise she said that she would have to think about it! My pride was dented. The next day, however, she approached me and said she would be pleased to come. My problem was solved and my pride restored. I gathered subsequently that she was annoyed at her colleagues for contacting me. It turned out that June was a good dancer, and we had an enjoyable evening.

Life at Sandiway House had a rhythm, and it seemed that it would go on beating like that forever, although I knew I would have to leave one day, because I was at the beginning of my career. It all came to an end quite suddenly through my first experience of reorganization. Our area office had merged with another, with the new entity being based in Chester. I had no objection to Chester; it was, after all, where I had attended school for ten years, but it was 20 miles from home. Job-wise I wasn't affected because I was a head office resource, and I went where I was sent. But I was concerned about Cliff and Arthur, who were interviewed along with their peers in the other area to see who would get the new higher-rated job, a process with which I would become very familiar in the years to come. For some time our office focused on little else but reorganization, and we analyzed every announcement that came out from our head office. I was glad when Cliff and Arthur were both successful, and Harry and John also received promotions. I was reassigned to Chester almost immediately.

I have very fond memories of Sandiway House, partly no doubt because of nostalgia, but partly because it was a symbol of a system that recognized and valued individuals and the roles they played in the overall success of the enterprise. I never quite experienced again that sense of belonging, but I always tried, when I had the opportunity, to create some of the same atmosphere in the work units for which I became responsible.

5

THE HYPNOTIST

Sport for me can be summed up in three words: soccer, golf, cricket. Comparing the three is difficult because they are so very different, but cricket and golf have two important characteristics in common, characteristics that none of the other major popular sports seem to have. First, they are both games where honour, integrity, and sportsmanship are critical, and secondly, there is an important social component. After the game is won or lost, rivalries are forgotten, or at least put aside, and the players usually gather for a discussion about the ebb and flow of the game, the good shots and the bad shots—all accompanied by good-natured banter and, of course, a drink or two. There is no real comparison between cricket and soccer save they are both team games. To use a music analogy, if soccer is a pop song, cricket is a symphony.

My cricket career began in our own backyard, where my brother, Graham, and I had endless test matches on the lawn. He had a bat autographed by the flamboyant Denis Compton, and I had one signed by his rival, the dour Yorkshireman, Len Hutton. Our lawn had designated scoring values. We ran for any runs arising from a ball staying within the confines of the lawn. A ball hit on the flower beds was an automatic boundary, and a ball hit into the gardens either side was a six—but the latter had the disadvantage that the batsman responsible had to retrieve the ball while hoping that it hadn't broken any windows or garden frames in the process. Occasionally windows were broken, including our own, but our parents were remarkably calm about it, perhaps recognizing that it was the price they paid for hours of friendly sibling play.

I continued with cricket when I joined the King's school in Chester and played for the school team. After leaving school, on Saturdays I played for Northwich, the local town team. On Sundays and in mid-week knockout competitions, I played with Chester Crossbatters, a team made up of old boys from the King's School, of which I was, of course, one.

In the '60s, Chester Crossbatters had an array of cricketing talent to draw on, including a former Captain of England Schoolboys and several players who had played county cricket. Apart from being a very competitive cricket team, we had considerable camaraderie, because we all knew each other very well and had similar backgrounds. Our Sunday cricket matches were a lot of fun, and players took their wives or girlfriends, sometimes mothers and fathers, and occasionally children, to have a fun day out at cricket clubs on Merseyside, across Cheshire, and parts of Shropshire and North Wales. We didn't have a home ground of our own and were a visiting team, but occasionally we borrowed a ground for a "home" fixture.

In 1967 I was captain of our team, responsible for the tactical decisions on the field, including field placement, the disposition of the bowlers, and the batting order. Off the field, as captain I had a responsibility to help create a pleasant atmosphere within our own team and with the other teams we played, because these were friendly matches. I took this responsibility seriously.

On Sunday, August 27 of that year, we played at Hightown, near Southport in Lancashire. I am sure of the day because I still have the cricket calendar for that season. The day was one of those all too frequent in England, quite cool, overcast, and threatening rain throughout the day. In fact, much to everyone's surprise, it never did rain, and we completed the game around our usual finishing time of 6:30. I don't remember who won; it may have even been a draw, but I am sure we had a good game.

Hightown has a very pleasant ground and clubhouse, and we looked forward to a fun evening after we had showered and changed. Once in the bar we relaxed, the first couple of pints slipping down easily, perhaps too easily. In those days, the social mores and the driving and drinking laws were regrettably not up to the standards of today, but the roads were quieter, the cars slower, and that, combined with some luck, got us home safely. We chatted with the other team about the game. Usually after we had loosened up, the stories would come out, perhaps a heated discussion or two about a contentious umpire's ruling in the day's play or some other aspect of cricket. This evening something different happened. The captain of the Hightown team went to the centre of the room and cupped his hands round his mouth.

"I am pleased to announce that this evening," he bellowed in the style of a music hall announcer, "we have been able to attract a famous hypnotist to demonstrate his hypnotic powers." The Crossbatters looked at each other and smiled in anticipation, wondering what we were in for. "Ladies and gentlemen," the captain continued, "I give you"—his voice rising to a crescendo—"Mesmerist!" He waved to one side, and out from the changing room, to generous applause, came someone we quickly recognized, mainly because of his height and beard, as the opening fast bowler—only he wasn't dressed in his cricket gear. A checked tablecloth was wrapped around him like a cape, and he wore a straw hat. At best it was a rudimentary disguise, but we were an easy audience to please and we were very pleased.

"Thank you, ladies and gentlemen, and fellow cricketers," he began. "I am going to show you my powers of hypnosis. First, with a member of the Hightown team," he said, looking around. "I pick you," he said, pointing to a member of his team, the wicket keeper, who looked a bit reluctant but came forward nevertheless.

"Thank you, James, for volunteering," Mesmerist said, motioning for him to sit down on a chair. "First, I must ask that you obey all the instructions I give you. Do that and you will come to no harm." James nodded. Mesmerist produced a large, shining gold watch.

"I want you to watch this watch," he said, and we sniggered over his little pun. "Specifically, I want you to watch the second hand go round and round for a minute." More sniggering. "Please concentrate. Do not look at anything else. Watch the second hand go round and round and round." James focused his eyes on the watch.

After a minute or so, Mesmerist said in a monotonic voice, "Now, James, you are very tired. Your eyelids are heavy. I want you to close your eyes. When I ask you to open them, you will do exactly as I say." James did as he was told. "Please get up from the chair and walk around the room," instructed Mesmerist. James obeyed the instructions, keeping a straight face, while everyone else was trying to make him laugh. Then Mesmerist went through a number of other similar commands, and James complied with all of them. The two of them were putting on a good show. Finally, Mesmerist said, "Return to your seat. When I snap my fingers, you will be awake." James sat down. Mesmerist snapped his fingers, and James opened his eyes and shook himself as though he had been in a trance.

Mesmerist took a big bow, and we all clapped and cheered. This was fun, and we wondered what would come next.

"I would now like a volunteer from the Crossbatters team," Mesmerist said when the raucous applause died down. I can't remember whether I volunteered of my own will or was pushed, but if the latter, I certainly didn't mind. It was, after all, part of my job as captain to foster harmonious relations. Mesmerist came up to me and shook my hand, putting his left hand round my neck, pulling me closer, and winking as he did so.

"Please be a good sport," he said quickly and softly in my ear. I understood him right away. He was a fake, just as I'd thought. But I am nothing if not a good sport and was happy to play along. When Mesmerist asked me to sit down, I did so willingly. He went through the same preamble as he had with James, except that he asked me to keep my eyes shut the whole time. I thought to myself, *At least this makes it a little easier to keep a straight face, because I won't see the others trying to make me laugh.* On his command, I stood up with what I hoped was a very trance-like expression on my face. It was, at least, my best effort, because I was trying so hard to be an effective straight man for him.

"And now, Chris," Mesmerist intoned, "please walk five paces to your left." That was easy, I thought. "Now six paces to the right. Turn around." I followed his instructions to the letter, feeling increasingly proud of my efforts in giving everybody a good time.

"I would now like you to do some Irish dancing. You can do that, can't you? Please nod your head if you can." I nodded my head, although this was many years before anyone had heard of Michael Flatley and *Riverdance*, but I had seen some Irish dancing on television and proceeded, on his command, to give the best rendition I could. I must have been quite good, or at least credible, because the audience in the bar loved it and cheered me on. Everyone, including me, was enjoying themselves. I wished I could see them, but I was determined to keep my end of the bargain by keeping my eyes shut, as I had been instructed.

"That's enough," Mesmerist said, seeing I was getting a little tired. "Now I want you to take a rest. Please lie down on the floor." I obeyed his instructions. "Pease raise and lower your left arm." I did. "Please raise your right arm." I did. After my Irish dancing I had no difficulty with these simple instructions, and the gathering seemed to be enjoying it even more, so I took no small pleasure in performing for their enjoyment. "Please raise your left leg." I did. "Now your right leg." I lifted my leg as I'd been told, and by now the laughter was very loud, although I could not account for why it should be so. "Hold it there," Mesmerist said, and I did, feeling the strain a little in my muscles, tired as they were after the day's cricket. Next thing I felt was a rush of cold liquid as he emptied a large jug of water down my pant leg. I was soaked. I had been had—well and truly had! The audience, including my own team, was in stitches of laughter. But Mesmerist wasn't finished with me.

"Now he is awake," he said, "and a little wet, let me ask him one question. Would you have allowed this to happen if you had known what was coming?"

"Of course not," I blurted, feeling a little foolish.

"So that proves it, ladies and gentlemen! You heard from the man himself. He must have been hypnotized!" Mesmerist declared to the assembled throng as he twirled around with one hand raised in the air in a triumphant flourish.

6

A GOOD DECISION

"My name's Barry Behrend," said the man, of medium height with Laurence-Harvey features, who approached me as I emerged from the arrivals lounge at Toronto airport on Good Friday, 1969, after my flight from Manchester. "You must be Chris. I thought I'd come to meet you. I'll drive you downtown," was all delivered in a southern England accent that I couldn't pinpoint exactly but which I later learned was from Essex.

"Thanks very much. That's very kind of you," I said, because I wasn't expecting anyone to meet me. I hadn't met Barry before, but his name was familiar to me. Barry was the manager of the department at Ontario Hydro that had recently hired me. The process of emigration hadn't taken long. I'd seen an advert in the English newspapers for computer specialists. I didn't meet those requirements, but I replied anyway, describing my qualifications and experience. Soon afterwards I was interviewed in London by Geoff Brown, also an Englishman, who spoke glowingly of Hydro as a company and Canada as a country.

After that I had a medical examination. I was still recovering from an abscess that had developed following two operations to treat appendicitis the year before, but I felt fit. The medical seemed to go satisfactorily, so I thought no more about it. Shortly thereafter I received an offer. The job at Ontario Hydro was ideal, with an attractive salary and some moving expenses. I accepted the offer immediately, and then I had to notify a company in Halifax, Nova Scotia, to turn down their offer, which I had accepted after turning down a job offer in Cambridge, England.

I had felt the need for a change, even for a while. I had lived in Cheshire all my life, had attended university at nearby Manchester, and was working at the same company for which my father had worked for 35 years. The farewells to friends and family had all been completed over the past few days, and my mother had driven me to Manchester airport earlier in the day for what was to be my first-ever flight. Although it was difficult for both of us, my mother was very supportive and understood my reasons for going.

"Where's your luggage?" Barry asked now, looking around.

"Coming on the next flight," I replied. I had changed planes very quickly in London, and I had been warned that my luggage might be delayed, in which case it would be delivered to my hotel room when it arrived.

As Barry drove me from the airport, I looked around. Everywhere was that drab grey-brown colour of early spring, in stark contrast to the very green England I had just left. And like most immigrants, I couldn't help but notice the preponderance of overhead wires in my new country. Hydro had booked me into the Waldorf Astoria on Charles Street, which sounded quite opulent when I first heard about it. Reality didn't quite meet those high expectations, but it was perfectly adequate for me. The luggage came a few hours later, as promised, while I was asleep, trying to shake off a cold that I had picked up playing golf in the rain the day before. The first couple of days I stayed in the hotel, trying to get better. On the third day, the telephone rang.

"Hi, Chris, it's Barry. Would you like to come and have dinner with us this evening?" I accepted. Barry picked me up, and I went and met his wife, Valerie, and their three young children: Robin, Bruce, and Alison. After dinner, during which I had my first taste—and probably my second and third—of Barry's homemade wine, we played Scrabble while three-year-old Alison was trying to tickle my feet under the table, which gave me an excuse for coming in last. Barry then drove me back to the hotel.

Hydro had allowed me a few days to get my bearings around the city and to find accommodation, but I used those days to get completely better. When I reported for work, one of Barry's subordinates, Ray Williams, helped me orient myself within the company. Ray told me that Geoff Brown, the man who had interviewed me in London, was now planning to return to the United Kingdom. *That's odd. What does he know that I don't know?* I thought to myself. I never really found out.

I learned from Ray about the bells that were rung at Hydro: at 8:30, when work started; before lunch; and at 4:30, when work stopped. This, of course, was long before any notion of flexible hours. "If you are late,"

Ray warned me, "time clerks will be waiting to take your name." I was horrified and vowed that I would never be caught that way. Some of the other rules and regulations were stricter than I had been accustomed to, and I wondered what kind of company I had joined. I needn't have had any fears. This was the first day of what turned out to be a very fulfilling and rewarding 32-year career in a very progressive company.

At that time, Hydro had staff in offices across the city, and I was assigned to a group working at the Manulife building on Bloor Street. Barry was based on University Avenue, but he would pop in occasionally to see how I was getting along. One day he said, "Do you play cricket?"

"I do," I replied.

"Great!" he said. "There's a game at Stratford on Sunday." The team was called the Stage Cricket Club; it had been founded originally by a group of English actors who wanted something to do in their off times. Over time, others like Barry had been added. My immediate supervisor and friend, Dave, had also been invited to play, and together we drove down to Stratford. Our opponents were a team of Stratford actors, captained by that Stratford icon Mervyn "Butch" Blake. In those days there were no plays on Sundays, and after the game, played in the idyllic setting by the theatre on the banks of the Avon, Butch took us on a tour of the theatre. Dave and I performed moderately well in the afternoon game and were asked to continue playing, which we did—in my case, for many years. Not long after the Stratford match, Barry popped his head into my office.

"Do you play golf?" he asked.

"I do," I replied.

"Great!" he said. "Can you play on Wednesday afternoon?" Dave and I arranged to take the afternoon off, and we had an enjoyable game, followed by drinks and dinner at Barry's. At the time, Barry was into making homemade beer, and we had been selected for the first tasting. The beer went down well, very well indeed. We commented on how tasty it was, but I think that reflected the strength of the beer! Somehow we got home that night. The next day, both Dave and I were feeling a little fragile but not too much the worse for wear. We chuckled later that day when we heard that Barry had to leave the office early because he was not well.

The friendship with Barry and his family continued. When Ena came on the scene from Scotland, she was welcomed as well, and Valerie and Ena attended cooking classes together; we all played badminton for a while, then bridge, and so on.

In late 1971 Ena was expecting our first child, and we had decided to go back to the United Kingdom. The hardest part was telling friends like Barry and Valerie of our decision. We sold our furniture and car and moved into a furnished apartment. Lisa was born in June, and she was seriously ill with meningitis, contracted at birth. The resulting impact on us, and our uncertainty about employment in Britain, caused us to reconsider our plans to return to the United Kingdom. Although it was difficult telling our parents we had changed our minds, it was great to tell our friends. Barry and Valerie were especially helpful when our baby was born. I remember one evening when Ena and I had been looking for a house, Barry paced the floor with Lisa—only weeks old—in his arms, trying to comfort her.

Over the years we have remained close friends—they are a part of our family, because as immigrants one does not have family close by—and have enjoyed many happy times together. Not long ago, we entertained Barry and Valerie. As we were having a predinner drink and some appetizers, and bringing each other up to date with the goings on in our respective families, Barry said, quite out of the blue, "You know, I must say that I feel somewhat responsible for all that has happened."

"What do you mean? Ena asked.

"I mean the development of your whole family, through you and Chris, your children, and now the grandchildren."

"I still don't understand," Ena said.

"Well," said Barry, "a long time ago, there was an Englishman who applied to join Hydro, and I thought he was suitable. I also noticed from his application that he played cricket, and I thought to myself he might be useful, as the Stage was short of players." We all knew, of course, who he was talking about. "The only problem was," continued Barry, "the personnel department recommended that he not be hired, on the basis of the medical report, as it raised possible long-term health concerns that might have an impact on the company. I considered this carefully, because it wasn't easy to reject advice from that quarter. However, the recommendation didn't make sense to me, and I was annoyed at personnel for interfering, anyway, so I ignored the advice and hired Chris," he said, looking at me.

He had never mentioned this to us before, and the implications took a while to sink in. "And then, when I met you that Easter weekend, and you had that terrible cold, I worried a little and wondered briefly whether personnel had been right, after all. But after that you were fine. I look back on it now, more than 40 years later, and take a good deal of pleasure from it. It was," he said with a satisfied smile, "a good decision." Ena and I quickly concurred. Barry held up his hand. He hadn't finished.

"Furthermore," he said, chuckling, "the Stage won a lot more games as a result!"

Barry and Valerie Behrend, 1961, at Niagara Falls

7

HELP!

After I had been in Canada for three weeks, I rented my first apartment—Apartment 905, to be exact—in a brand-new building on the southwest corner of Davisville and Mount Pleasant, one of the many apartment buildings that were being built at that time in Toronto. I had looked at a few places, but I liked the Davisville area, and it was an easy subway ride to work. The apartment, a bachelor, cost $141 a month. I thought about getting a one-bedroom apartment, but they were $20 more, and I took the smaller one to be prudent, although by today's standards it was quite large.

Immediately on the left going into the apartment was a door leading to a small dressing room, which in turn led through another door to the bathroom. The living/dining/bedroom was L-shaped. I had been overwhelmed at the prospect of buying some furniture and had limited funds, so I opted for a deal at a Queen Street furniture store where I could pick up all I needed for about $1,000. My bed was a chesterfield, vivid blue in colour, which was moderately comfortable as a bed at night but was neither comfortable nor stylish as a couch by day. I had a round table and four chairs, some side tables, and a shelving unit with a black metal frame and teak shelves, which displayed some books that had recently arrived in a trunk from England. I also had a small television. The kitchen came with a fridge and a stove, and I bought pans and cutlery from Eatons.

The apartment also had a large balcony off the living area, which overlooked a park, so there was always some activity going on. It was only a short walk to the subway, and I could be downtown within minutes to Manufacturers Life Insurance Company on Bloor Street, where I was first assigned—and where work began at 8:30 precisely. At the top of the building there was a pool and sundeck, which I used quite frequently.

Underground there was a garage, although I didn't have a car to begin with. There was also a laundry room, and I wished I had listened more closely to my mother's instructions on laundry! Usually I just threw everything in together. All in all, it wasn't exactly home, but it was a reasonable way in which to start my new life in Canada.

One Friday morning, about three months after moving in, I woke at my usual time of seven, looking forward to the day ahead, but more especially to the weekend to follow. I rose, folded up my bed (a habit at which my mother and Ena would be totally astonished), and went into the dressing room, where I selected my clothes for the day—not that there was much to pick from. A shirt and tie were the usual variables in my dress to accompany a sports jacket, blazer, or suit, and I grabbed some underwear and socks from the built-in drawers. Having decided on my ensemble, I went into the bathroom and shut the door. There was, of course, no reason to shut the door, since I was alone, but it was force of habit. As I closed it I heard a click; I thought nothing of it at the time. I shaved and showered, towelled myself down, and went to open the door to get dressed. I pulled the doorknob. It came off in my hands. That surprised me, certainly, but I wasn't immediately perturbed, and I examined what was left. It never occurred to me that there would be a problem. I thought there would be something else I could pull or push and the door would open, but there wasn't—the door was well and truly locked.

Darn, I said to myself, or words to that effect. And then I laughed at my predicament. *There must be an easy way out of this,* I thought. I examined the handle and tried to replace it, but that didn't work. I looked round for something to insert between the jamb and the latch. I rummaged through the drawers; there hadn't yet been time for the usual assortment of items to accumulate. All that I had was a comb, but that was too thick.

Don't panic, I thought. *Just sit down and think it through.* At least I had the toilet as a seat, although I decided to put the lid down on the seat and sit on that. It wasn't as comfortable as the seat, and it was a little cold for my bottom, so I wrapped the towel, still fairly wet in parts, round me and sat down. I had nothing to read but the writing on the tube of toothpaste and bottle of shampoo, which took me all of two minutes, and that was it. I looked around the bathroom. There were no windows, and the length of the bathroom was along the inside of the corridor so the wall was thick enough to accommodate the water and drainage pipes. I had never heard any noise from the apartments to either side of me.

I wondered what the time was. It must be about seven thirty now, approaching the time I usually left for work, and from now on the corridor would be used by other tenants walking to the elevator. Perhaps if I tried banging on the door and the wall I might attract some attention. First I used my fists; for a few minutes I banged away. There was no response, although I could hear the sound of one or two doors closing. Even if anyone heard some banging, he or she likely wouldn't think anything of it or do anything about. In my limited experience, once in an apartment building, people generally kept very much to themselves.

I cheered myself up by reminding myself that at least I was locked in the bathroom, not out of it, and I had access to running water, of course. I could live here for a long time if I had to. And I might have to. I tested the door, wondering if I could break it down. I pushed it hard, but it was a solid door in a new building, and I couldn't get a run up to exert much force. The door refused to budge at all.

There's nothing else for it but to cry for help, I thought to myself. I wondered what I should say. "I'm locked in the bathroom!" seemed obvious. It was certainly factual, and I tried it several times. It sounded weird, perhaps because I wasn't in any immediate danger, as if I were about to fall over Niagara Falls. And although I tried to shout as loud as I could, I was conscious that my efforts didn't have the amount of desperation required to make it convincing or audible enough to a casual listener in the corridor. No one came to the door.

I then concluded that I should shout "Help!" I tried a couple of times, but I still couldn't bring myself to shout it with any conviction. I wasn't an endangered damsel in distress. I was a healthy young man locked, temporarily I hoped, in the bathroom. And then I remembered this was Friday. This was the day when people often left for the weekend right after work to get a head start on the traffic. They may have a cottage of their own, or their family might have one, or they might have an invitation to one, or they might be canoeing or visiting friends somewhere. It was possible that most of people on the floor would not be returning that day, and there might be nobody to hear my cries for help, weakening by the hour, all weekend!

Although this was disconcerting to me, I was far from panicking. I reminded myself again that, after all, I was safe and sound with lots of water and ready access to the bathroom. It was conceivable that I could go for many days before it became a major problem. But I didn't want it to go on for many days! I wanted it to stop right then and there, and this gave me the extra incentive I needed to shout "Help" more loudly and lustily than I had ever done before and, for that matter, ever since. I am sure I established a new personal best in loudness. But there was still no sign that my pleas had been heard. There was no knocking at the door or loud voices asking how I was.

How long would it be before someone came to look for me? I was due at work at 8:30 and was always prompt. Would my absence be noticed, and if so, would anyone do anything about it? Suppose I wasn't found at all? I hadn't even made a will yet, but on reflection, I consoled myself thinking that it wasn't much of a problem, since I had little assets to leave—and on further reflection, I decided that had failed to console me at all! I tried the "Help!" routine again and banged on the walls of the bathtub; it made a noise, but I think that unless you were immediately outside in the corridor you wouldn't have heard it.

The phone rang, and it kept ringing because I couldn't answer it. It was frustrating. It stopped and then 30 seconds later rang again. My hopes rose. I thought it might be Dave calling me from the office, perhaps wondering where I was. I had never been late before. There was nothing else to do but wait. About 20 minutes later I heard voices at the door, and a key was inserted in the lock. As someone came in, I could hear Dave's voice and another one. I shouted to them. "I'm locked in the bathroom!" Next thing, the bathroom door was opened, and I saw the superintendent, with Dave looking on behind.

"I was worried about you," said Dave, obviously relieved. "I thought something was wrong when you didn't show up this morning, but I had a devil of a job getting the superintendent to open the door for me."

"Good job you were, else it might have been awhile. Thanks for saving me!" I said.

The superintendent was fiddling with the door, pretending to ignore Dave's criticism. "I don't understand how this could have happened," he said. "You shouldn't have locked the door in the first place."

"I didn't," I retorted. "The handle came off in my hands." Disbelievingly, to simulate what I had done, he went into the bathroom himself, closed the door, and found he couldn't open the door either!

"I'll have it fixed right away," he said sheepishly as we let him out, though it was very tempting to leave him there.

The moral of the story is, of course: Punctuality Pays—unless you take a toolkit with you every time you go to the bathroom!

8

"You'll Never Meet Anyone in a Bar"

The older generation has always seen it as their prerogative to give advice to the younger generation. The advice is usually well-intentioned but is often advice that they didn't follow themselves when they were young.

There is a wonderful Somerset Maugham story about a father who dispenses some advice to his son, who is about to go to Monte Carlo on his own to play in a tennis tournament. The three pieces of advice are: don't gamble, don't lend money, and don't have anything to do with women. The boy ignores the advice, or more precisely, perhaps, is not able to follow it, and he returns home having fortuitously made a lot of money. The father is worried he has lost all credibility for any future advice he might give to his son. His friends try to cheer him up. "Don't worry," they say. "It is better to be born lucky than clever or rich."

There is one piece of advice that is often passed down from generation to generation. At one time or another most of us have received it from our parents or passed it on to our children. The advice is "You'll never meet anyone in a bar." The implied inference, of course, is that you will never meet anyone respectable of the opposite sex in such an establishment. It seems to be a kind of universally accepted truth that nothing good can come of two people meeting in this way. When you think about it, the statement is illogical. Why is it that if a respectable man goes to a bar it is axiomatic that any woman he meets there is *not* respectable, and vice versa? If that were the case, bars would be empty.

I was at work one morning in August 1969, when Dave, whose desk was directly behind mine, said, "Interested in going out tonight? I've been given free tickets to go to the Blue Orchid."

"I've never heard of it. What is it?" I queried.

"It's some kind of bar," Dave clarified. That was enough for me.

"Why not?" I said.

Dave had several free tickets, and we asked Shawn and John to join us. All of us were Englishmen in our mid to late twenties and recently recruited by Ontario Hydro to work on a new computer system. Dave had been in Toronto about a year, but the rest of us had been here for just a few months. Dave and I had quickly hit it off and became friends. We had a lot in common. We played cricket and golf together and enjoyed discussing politics and reminiscing about the old country together. I had visited his home several times to meet his wife and their new baby daughter. Shawn and John had arrived in advance of their wives and families and were looking round for permanent accommodation. I was single and had just moved into an apartment. Tragically, John was later to commit suicide.

Early in the evening we went to the Blue Orchid. None of us had been there before. It was located on the south side of Bloor, just west of Yonge. On the sign outside it was billed as a "speakeasy," not because of any linkage to the prohibition era but to capitalize on the more liberal behaviours then sweeping through Toronto ("the good," but not so good, anymore). Our free passes worked, and we went inside. Basically it was a very large room, similar to a German beer hall. The décor was very plain, and there were rows of long wooden tables with benches on either side. It was only about seven thirty, but already the place was busy; it was obviously popular. We sat down at a table and were soon approached by a waiter wearing a shirt with rolled-up sleeves, a cap, and an apron with a pocket for carrying cash. He carried adroitly above his head a large, round tray, on top of which were glasses of draft beer, one dollar each.

We quickly quaffed our first beers, which were replenished by the waiter who miraculously appeared with another tray just at the right moment. The place was filling up. The music was loud with popular songs from the '60s, making conversation a little difficult. This didn't stop John, the technical wizard amongst us, from attempting to start a work-related discussion. "I think we should consider online updating of the main file," he said, "rather than batch updating."

"That would take too long to develop," said Dave, ever the pragmatist, dismissing the proposition. "And besides, we we're here to enjoy ourselves," he said, downing his second beer as if to prove it.

At the far end of the room was a stage with a curtain, and I wondered what it was for. Around eight thirty we found out. A man emerged from behind the curtain; he was dressed as the waiters were. He stretched out his hands to quiet us.

"Welcome to the Blue Orchid," he bellowed without the aid of a microphone. "I hope you all have a great evening. Now it's time for the singalong." He then reached up and pulled on a rope, which unfurled a screen, before he retreated behind the curtain. The music started, several decibels higher than before.

I think I'm gonna be sad, I think it's today, yeah/The girl that's driving me mad is going away . . .

Through the smoke-filled air, a beam of light from a projector lit up the screen, and the words of the Beatles' song appeared. This made it easy for us to sing along. And sing along we did. It was made even easier by the bouncing ball that highlighted the next word to sing.

She's got a ticket to ride/She's got a ticket to ride . . .

After that song, the words of "When the Red, Red Robin . . ." came up. We chuckled at the appearance of this old song, but we sang along anyway, entering into the spirit. They were interspersing some old songs with contemporary ones. We noticed some of the others were standing up and swaying and dancing to the music. Our inhibitions were going fast, and we were enjoying ourselves.

"When the red, red robin comes bob, bob bobbin' along, along," we warbled at the top of our voices. We were having a good time. We noticed that the more beer we drank the better we sang. John mumbled something about the beneficial effects of lubrication on the larynx, but we didn't pay him much attention.

Then the girls appeared. There were five of them. We made room for them at the end of our table and we exchanged, as one does, pleasantries and quick introductions before continuing as before.

Cheer up, cheer up, the sun is red/Live, love, laugh, and be happy . . .

I'm not very good at remembering names, but I think there were Barbara, Jennifer, Susie, Rosemary, and Ena. I happened to sit by Rosemary, who was a pretty girl with dark hair and a trim figure.

"Have you come here before?" I asked, trying to break the ice.

"Oh yes," she said, "I've come here quite often. It's a lot of fun," giving what I have to say was a very nice smile, and then more of the Beatles drowned out any further conversation for the moment.

She loves you, yeah, yeah, yeah/She loves you yeah, yeah, yeah . . .

What a great song! By now most people in the room were on their feet. Some climbed onto the chairs, including Rosemary and me. The whole room was alive. I saw a few people climbing onto the tables, but they were quickly discouraged by staff—not, it seemed, because they would damage the tables but out of concern for safety.

And you know you should be glad . . .

I began dancing with Rosemary, or more exactly, alongside her. I couldn't help but notice that Rosemary was a good dancer. Nor could I fail to notice the bare midriff prominently displayed as she gyrated in time to the music. So far we seemed to be getting on just fine. What an unexpected bonus to an evening out with the boys, I thought.

In moments between songs, I noticed Dave was talking to one of the other girls, Ena, a tall girl with shoulder-length, fair hair. Dave was quite garrulous and could be a lot of fun. He could also relax this night, because I was driving him home. I gathered from the Scottish burr that Ena was from Scotland, and from brief snippets of conversation I gleaned the information that she was on vacation, visiting her brother.

"What do you do?" I asked Rosemary when there was a momentary pause in the music.

"I work in an office downtown," she said gloomily. Then her eyes sparkled, as she added "but I would like to be a belly dancer!" I was a bit taken aback. I had never come across a would-be belly dancer before. It seemed incredible, but I was sure she was sincere. Although I am not well qualified in the art—or is it a science?—of belly dancing, I was certain, based on what I had seen so far, that she would make a fine belly dancer—probably one of the finest in the whole of Metropolitan Toronto, if not further afield, if she were to put her mind to it. It should have turned me on, I suppose, but it didn't. Whatever interest I had felt toward Rosemary to that point waned somewhat. I didn't drop Rosemary, but I thought I should hedge my bets. I turned to participate in the conversation Dave and Ena were having. Since Dave was married, I could hardly be accused of butting in.

"What do you do?" I asked Ena when I got the chance. This wasn't the first thing I usually asked girls on meeting them, but I suppose I was still thinking of my exchange with Rosemary. For a moment I wondered if they were a troupe of exotic dancers having a night off, on a busman's holiday, as it were.

"I teach mathematics," she said.

That's quite a bit different from belly dancing, I thought. "How did you meet the other girls?" I asked, curious as to how Ena and Rosemary had met, wondering what mathematics and belly dancing could possibly have in common.

"I met Barbara on the plane when I was coming over, and I gave her my phone number. She said she would call me sometime. She called me today, and here I am. I haven't met Rosemary before." That explained it.

It was difficult to get more than an odd word in because Dave was monopolizing the conversation. I got my chance when Dave left to go to the washroom. Then the music started again, and the familiar words flashed on the screen.

Hey Jude, don't make it bad/Take a sad song and make it better . . .

What a terrific song! Being born and bred 35 miles from Merseyside, I felt quite at home. Ena wasn't as good a dancer as Rosemary, but she had a nice way about her, and I liked her long hair. She liked the Beatles, too.

Remember to let her into your heart/Then you can start to make it better, better, better . . .

This was indeed much better. We both knew the words to the song and didn't need the bouncing ball. I was sorry when the song ended.

The girls then decided to go en masse to the ladies' room, and Ena disappeared with them. By this time Shawn and John had gone, and there were just Dave and me, feeling very mellow, and we laughed at how the evening had turned out to be much more pleasant than we had imagined.

We then noticed Ena standing before us. "Do you know where the others are? They left the washroom before me," she asked. Dave and I looked around. We couldn't see them.

"They must have gone," said Dave.

"But I've got to get back to Willowdale," she said, looking a little worried.

"Don't worry," I said in a flash. "I can drive you. I have to drive Dave home, anyway." At this she seemed relieved, perhaps partly because of the offer and perhaps partly because of the reassurance that Dave's presence would represent.

And so we left the Blue Orchid. In today's circumstances I would not have dreamed of driving a car, but in those days, regrettably, it was different. We found my car, and I very deliberately drove to Dave's home, a delightful coach house that he rented in Rosedale. Dave gave Ena a friendly kiss as he left the car, and I proceeded north to Willowdale. I had a pleasant chat with Ena in the car. She was staying with her brother, and she told me about some of his eccentricities, particularly about his habit of playing tricks on her. It showed she had a sense of humour, and I warmed to her.

"When are you going back to Scotland?" I said.

"In a week's time," she replied.

What the heck, I thought. "Would you have dinner with me tomorrow night?" I blurted out.

"Yes," she said.

"I'll pick you up about eight o'clock." And that was that.

She did indeed return to Scotland a week later, but we corresponded, in letters we still have today, and she subsequently came out to Canada. We were married within 18 months, and now, 40 years later, have two children, two children-in-law, and four grandchildren. I have always been a bit vague to them about how I met their respective mother and Nana. Now I must confess that I did indeed meet her in a bar! I suppose the exception must prove the rule.

I never went to the Blue Orchid again. It must have closed shortly thereafter.

I wonder what ever happened to Rosemary.

Nine people who would not be in this picture had I not met
Ena in that bar! July 2009. Back row: Martin, Janice, me,
Ena, Lisa, Mark. Front Row: Tyler, Damon, Luke, Liam

Ena and me, 1970

9

THE DANCING LESSONS

Bob came to work at Ontario Hydro as a computer programmer with Dave and me in 1970, to help us develop a new customer billing system. Bob was well qualified. He had a degree in computer science and had taken a number of programming courses, but he had little experience, and this was his first job.

The first thing I noticed about him was his smile. He had one of those big, broad smiles that can light up a room. We took to him immediately. He was a cheerful hard worker and was very determined, a great asset in programming. But he could also be stubborn, which, fortunately as it happens, isn't a great liability in that line of work. Often I looked up from my own desk to see him, obviously dejected, with his head resting on his hands, reviewing errors in his program that had been identified by the computer. That mood never lasted for long. After a few moments you would see him grit his teeth as he tried again to get it right. And he usually succeeded in the end, because he didn't like asking for help. He was also well read, and whenever the opportunity arose, he enjoyed debating political issues or topics of current interest. Sometimes Dave or I would take extreme positions just to get him going, but as soon he realized it, "You're just kidding me, right?" he would say, his face breaking into that wide smile, and we would have to admit that we were.

For lunch Dave and I usually purchased a boring sandwich from the deli on the ground floor of the building in which we worked, but a couple of times a week we went out to a local pub for a meat pie, with or without chips, and a beer. Occasionally we asked Bob to join us. We didn't have far to go, but we would have to walk more slowly than usual because Bob had trouble keeping up. He had suffered from cerebral palsy from birth. As a result, his arm and leg movements were laboured and restricted, and his speech was slow and slurred. We learned from him and from others how hard he had worked to overcome his limitations, and he told us of the long walks he took to improve his mobility. He had done remarkably well to achieve what he had, and we admired his tenacity, which also probably accounted for his stubbornness.

One morning, when Bob came in I noticed that something was wrong. Bob didn't have his usual smile or greeting. I waited until the coffee wagon came to our floor midmorning. "What's up?" I said.

"Nothing," he replied, looking surprised at my question.

"You don't look like your normal self," I ventured. Bob said nothing, collected his coffee, and went back to his desk. It wasn't like him. Later that morning he came over and sat by my desk.

"I do have a problem," he said and swallowed deeply, preparing himself. I thought it must be significant.

"Let's go to another room," I said, because it was difficult to hold a private conversation in our open office, and Bob's normal speaking voice was quite loud. We went down the corridor to a vacant office. We sat down and I looked at Bob.

"I'd give anything to be able to walk properly," he said, looking down at my legs, "like you." I nodded, wondering what was coming next. "You know how exercise helps my movements?" he went on. "Well, a few weeks ago I saw an advertisement in the paper for dancing lessons. It stressed that dancing was great exercise. So I went along to the studio." He told me the name of the studio, a well-known franchise. "I met this dance instructor and she gave me a private lesson. She said I danced really well, considering," he said. Bob and I knew what she meant by *considering*. "Anyway," Bob went on, "I went along for a second lesson, and she said she could see an improvement. She seemed nice and she thought that dancing would definitely help me, but it might take a long time, so I signed up for some lessons."

"I can see that they might help a bit," I said, thinking he was talking about a few lessons. I tried to sound encouraging. "How many have you signed up for?"

"Thirty-five hundred dollars' worth," he said. "Enough for three years of lessons." My jaw dropped. I was dumbfounded! "Thirty-five hundred dollars?" I repeated. "Have you paid any money?"

"She said it would be cheaper if I paid some in advance, so I took out a bank loan for $1,000, and I've signed a contract for the balance," Bob answered. "I know it sounds stupid, but I thought it would be worth it if it helped. But the more I think of it, I'm not sure I've done the right thing," he continued. "I got carried away," he said, smiling sheepishly.

I was staggered. The whole idea seemed ludicrous. This was 1970 and $3,500 was a lot of money, probably equivalent to at least $25,000 in today's dollars. Taking advantage of Bob in this way seemed such a cheap trick, and I wondered whether a lack of female companionship might also have been a factor in his decision, though I didn't pursue that with Bob.

"I don't know what I can do, but I'd like to help. Can I talk to Dave about it?" was all I could bring myself to say. Bob liked Dave and said that was fine. When I explained the situation to Dave, he felt as shocked and indignant as I, and we discussed possible actions. We decided that, if Bob agreed, we would approach the bank and the dancing studio in an effort to cancel the contracts. We explained to Bob what we proposed to do. He really didn't want to cause any fuss, but after further discussion, he said he would like to recover his money and authorized us to contact the bank and the studio on his behalf.

The bank manager was reluctant to see us until we convinced him we had Bob's authorization. We outlined the situation. The manager was sympathetic but unyielding.

"He took out a personal loan; he could have used it for anything, and certainly he never mentioned anything about dancing lessons. I'm sorry, but I can't do anything." We were disappointed, but we could see it from the bank's perspective.

The next day we went along to the studio. It was on the second floor of a commercial building, and as we climbed the stairs we could hear dance music. We noticed various promotions and event notices on the walls. At the top of the stairs, we entered the lobby and bumped into a good-looking woman in a sequined dress, who was probably in her late thirties. She might have been the dancing instructor Bob had been seeing, but we couldn't be sure, and we weren't about to tell her our mission. We asked to see the manager. She didn't ask why but led us down a short corridor, knocked on the door, and opened it before hearing any reply.

We introduced ourselves to the man behind the desk. He confirmed that he was "in charge," and asked us why we there. Again we described the problem and our proposed solution in view of the special circumstances—tearing up Bob's contract. As we talked, he swivelled on his chair to open a filing cabinet, from which he drew a file. He flipped over the pages. When we had finished, he closed the file, crossed his arms on it, and leaned towards us. "Look," he said, "he signed the contract of his own free will. I don't know if the dancing lessons will help him, but they certainly won't do any harm. So what's the problem? I have a business to run." He was dismissing us.

Dave rose to his feet. He was more than six feet tall, and he pointed a finger at the man. "I think that what you have done is despicable," he told him. "You have preyed on a vulnerable young man. I can tell you that Bob isn't going to pay any more money. Leave him alone. Furthermore, if you try to collect, we will go to the papers and let them have the full story. Think how that will affect your business."

With that, Dave brusquely turned around and walked out of the office. I followed quickly, neither of us listening to the protestations behind us. We reported back to Bob. Initially, he was concerned how far we had taken it.

"I appreciate what you've done," he said. "But I don't want any press coverage," he added quietly. He was worried that it would make him look foolish. "Maybe I should just pay the money and be done with it."

"Trust us," we reassured Bob. "He isn't going to take the chance of being publicly exposed."

The next few weeks were anxious ones for Bob, and we tried to keep his spirits up. He heard nothing from the dancing studio, and his confidence rose. We were sure he was free of that debt, although of course he was still liable for the bank loan. He was very grateful and thanked us profusely for our efforts.

Many months passed. One day, when Bob was back to his old self, I sidled up to him. "Signed up for any more lessons lately?" I said.

He looked back at me. "No need, Chris," he said. "I've learned my lesson," and out came that smile.

10

A Honeymoon, a Disaster, and a Tragedy

Oh Danny boy, the pipes, the pipes are calling
From glen to glen, and down the mountain side.
—Frederic Weatherly

"Do you want to come to the match the day after tomorrow?" asked Danny on New Year's Eve.

"Which match would that be?" I said obtusely, knowing full well who was playing.

"Why, the Celtic/Rangers game, of course," he replied. "It promises to be a cracker."

Nearly two weeks earlier, on December 19, 1970, Ena and I had been married in Glasgow. Ena had come from Canada several weeks earlier to make the arrangements and to satisfy the residence requirements for the reading of the banns. After the ceremony and a small reception attended by a few family members and friends, we escaped as soon as we could and drove in my brother's borrowed mini to Edinburgh for a brief honeymoon. Ena had taken pains to disguise the honeymoon destination and had used Dundee as the decoy. Such subterfuge probably wasn't necessary, but it worked. I hadn't been to Edinburgh before, and we enjoyed exploring the many historical and cultural amenities that the city offers from our base at the delightful Roxburghe Hotel, on Charlotte Square. Edinburgh remains one of our favourite places. We were there for just three days before we left to spend Christmas with my mother in Cheshire, some 225 miles away.

My mother was looking forward to us coming and made a number of preparations, one of which included pulling together the twin beds that my brother, Graham, and I had slept on for many years to create a double bed. The next morning, after a quick knock at the door, she

47

breezed in, as only she could, with cups of tea for us. On Christmas Eve, we visited Christine and Michael, my sister and brother-in-law, and their three children, who lived a half-hour drive away. During the evening it began to snow, and it was still snowing when we left. I drove slowly through the narrow, hedge-lined Cheshire lanes, partly because of the snow-covered roads and partly because I was still feeling the warm effects of the scotch I had savoured earlier. The tires crunched on the snow, and the car's headlights illuminated the flakes much like those glass toys when you shake them. We drove to attend midnight service at St. Vincent's in Knutsford, where to our delight, we saw that the church was lit by candles. During the service, attendants were on guard for renegade candles, which were soon extinguished. We had a very special Christmas that year.

On December 29 we said goodbye to my mother and took the train to Glasgow, where we had planned to spend New Year with Ena's parents before returning to Canada early in January. New Year in Scotland is an important occasion, more so than Christmas, and on New Year's Eve Ena's parents held a get-together with family and close friends. There was always a sing-song and lots of joke-telling on these occasions, with most contributing party pieces from their repertoire. I, not being very good at either, kept a low profile, but I enjoyed the celebrations.

Danny was there. He was the fiancé of Anne, Ena's younger sister. Danny was a "card" and the life and soul of every party. He had a pleasant tenor voice and of course "Danny Boy" was a much-requested song, but his specialty was jokes. He was quite a comedian, and he had one act that had us all roaring with laughter each time he performed it. Danny was tall and slim, and he would go into a corner of the room and wrap his long arms around his shoulders and back, pretending that he was in a passionate embrace with a woman and murmuring words of endearment as he did so. He was very funny.

Just after the "bells" at midnight, Ena and I—armed with our bottle, as is the custom—were preparing to leave to visit some of her friends. It was then that Danny asked me about the match. I hadn't seen Celtic or Rangers play before, except on television, and this seemed a great opportunity.

"D'you have tickets?" I asked, because I remembered reading in the *Glasgow Herald* that it was an all-ticket affair.

"No, but we can just pay at the gate," Danny said.

"Okay," I said, although I wasn't as confident as Danny that his plan would work and would still feel a little uncomfortable if it did. Danny picked me up on the morning of January 2. It was a damp, misty, cold day—a typical Glasgow winter's day.

"Let's pop into the pub for a quick one before the game," said Danny. We entered a pub near Ibrox Stadium, the home ground of Rangers in the south-west of the city, and Danny greeted his friends, who had gathered there by prior arrangement. None of them had tickets for the game.

"What'll you have?" Danny asked me.

"Pint of heavy," I replied, showing my newly acquired knowledge of beer terminology in Scotland. Danny went to the bar and returned with two pints and two shot glasses, which I realized were scotch chasers; they seemed to be an automatic accompaniment to a pint in those days. This was a big game for Danny and his friends, one of the biggest of the season, and important bragging rights were at stake. They chatted in eager anticipation over the prospects for the game. We downed the drinks quickly, as kickoff was approaching. We hadn't far to walk and headed to one end of the ground, where the Celtic supporters were destined to go. Most were wearing their green and white scarves or hats.

As we approached the turnstile, I became a little nervous. I had never tried to attend an all-ticket game before—or since, for that matter—without a ticket. Danny sensed my unease.

"Don't worry," he said. "Just give him the exact money, and he'll let you through. Follow me." He paid his money and went though the turnstile. I was next. With some trepidation, I went in and gave the money to the attendant. I couldn't look him in the eye, and for a brief moment I wondered if he would stop me entering, but he didn't bat an eyelid, and in a few seconds I was in the ground. There was now nothing to worry about, and I could relax, or so I thought. We picked our way up the terrace to a vantage point a little to one side behind one of the goals, where we stood in front of one of the metal barriers.

The stadium was packed, which was not surprising, since there were many, like Danny and I, who hadn't a ticket. I looked around. Many of the crowd was obviously the worse for wear and either hadn't recovered from Hogmanay or hadn't stopped celebrating it. The steps of the terrace were slippery, and it took me a while to realize they were running with urine. Some people couldn't reach the toilets in time or couldn't be bothered to try. This was no place for the faint-hearted! A few minutes before kickoff, I saw a meat pie fly through the air, landing on a man's head near the front. Meat pies don't, of course, fly by themselves. It had obviously been thrown, but it didn't seem to bother the target much. He turned around and, quickly concluding he couldn't possibly identify his assailant, proceeded to make the best of it by licking the remains of the pie from his face. I couldn't help but admire his *sangfroid*! I was an experienced soccer supporter and had attended many games to watch Manchester United, but I had never seen anything like this.

To be truthful, I remember very little about the game itself. Despite the derby atmosphere, it was a relatively dull game. Neither team scored, and there was nothing much to excite the crowd. As the game went on, I was looking forward to getting back to more comfortable surroundings. With about five minutes to go, Danny turned to me.

"We'd better leave now, so we don't get in the rush." I was only too happy to agree, and we pushed our way through the crowd to the exit without too much difficulty.

"Fancy a pint?" Danny said as we emerged from the stadium.

"Sure," I said, somewhat relieved the game was over and amenable to whatever he wanted to do.

"We'll get in the car and drive nearer home," he said. As we reached the car, we heard a huge roar. That'll be the end of the game," Danny said. "We've timed it just right."

We went to a pub not far from where Ena's parents lived. We talked, not about the game but about our respective futures while we finished our drinks.

"Want another one?" Danny said.

"No," I said, "We'd better get back." I was feeling concerned at leaving my new wife alone all afternoon. Just as we walked out through the pub, we heard some animated discussion about an accident at Ibrox, and people were gathered by the television. We thought nothing more about it. We assumed there had been the usual disturbances between rival supporters. Danny drove the short distance home. We had got within 10 yards of the front door when it opened. Ena and her mother greeted us with relief written on their faces.

"Where've you been? We've been worried about you!" said Ena.

"We had a quick pint after the game. What's the matter?" I said, wondering what could have possibly caused this level of concern.

"There's been a terrible crush at Ibrox, and lots of people have been injured. Some have died. When you didn't come back straight after the match, we were beginning to think the worst." She burst into tears. I put my arms around her and comforted her, as I heard the radio in the background giving further details.

Danny and I knew nothing about it. We didn't even know the final result. We quickly learned what had happened. In the last minute of the game, Celtic had scored. Many Rangers supporters, at the opposite end from where Danny and I had been standing, began to leave, disappointed at their team's apparent loss. No sooner had the game restarted then Rangers equalized. Those fans who were leaving the ground heard the roar of the crowd and began to retrace their steps back up the walkways to join in the celebration of the goal, only to meet fans hurrying out of the ground as the referee blew the whistle for the end of the game.

The result was a mess of tangled humanity. Sixty-six were killed, with many more injured, in what became known as the Ibrox disaster. Amongst them an eight-year-old boy, attending his first major soccer game with his stepfather, suffocated in the crush. No one should die from attending a football match! Of course I wondered, with perhaps a little guilt, to what extent the numbers of people in the ground without tickets had been a contributory factor, but no mention was made of that, at least in the reports I read.

Ena and I, unscathed and unscarred, returned to Canada the following day and were spared the unfolding of the anguish. Looking back, it seems surreal, as if I hadn't been there.

My memory of the disaster is inextricably linked to my memories of Danny, who became godfather to our daughter in 1972. Sadly, tragically, not long after that Danny was killed in a construction accident.

A honeymoon, a disaster, and a tragedy.

11

GRATTAN'S CATCH

Be not afraid of greatness: some are born great, some achieve greatness, and some have greatness thrust upon them.
—William Shakespeare

Recently escaped from a seminary and anxious to make up for lost time, Grattan O'Brien, born in St. Helens, that Anglo-Saxon bastion in North-West England, certainly fit the third category described by Shakespeare. Little did he—or anyone else, for that matter—know that by day's end, on that fateful July day in 1970, he would be a hero.

It was an unlikely scene for such heroism—a cricket pitch in southwest Ontario—and yet there were heroic connections, because the game was played in Woodstock, named after the town in Oxfordshire, near Blenheim. This was the Duke of Marlborough's palace, which was given to the Duke by a grateful English nation for his exploits against the French in the early 18th century.

Grattan had been picked to play for the Stage cricket team (which I have mentioned several times in other stories), although the word "picked" may be somewhat of a misnomer, for in truth, young Grattan wasn't much of a cricketer, and less generous folks would have described him as a "rabbit." However, Grattan did possess some qualities and redeeming features that made him attractive to the Stage. He was young, fit, and—most of all—he was available. He was also proud to turn out for the club.

The afternoon began uneventfully enough. The Stage batted first and was soon in trouble. Woodstock had a battery of young, lithe, fast bowlers who wreaked havoc and dismissed us all in short order for the meagre total of 25. Nothing more should be said about our woeful batting performance, and we were a chastened lot as we readied ourselves to take the field, rendered even more so because it was too early for tea and our stomachs were rumbling without the benefit of the cucumber sandwiches and fruitcake that were gracing the table in the pavilion. In spite of this, we were determined to try to restrict the Woodstock batting, even though we knew in our hearts of hearts it was a vain hope.

Woodstock's innings began briskly, with one of their opening batsmen in particularly good form. He quickly stroked a couple of boundaries, and our total was soon in sight. And then, just as we were about to give up all hope—indeed some of us had already waved goodbye to the last remnant of it as it slipped by—the unexpected happened.

Grattan's brother-in-law, John, a stalwart of the team for many years and a good all-rounder, began bowling an over. For some reason that I cannot recall, because it ran counter to the basic elements of cricket tactics, Grattan was fielding at "silly mid-on," which is perilously close to the batsman on the leg side, though it is not likely that Grattan knew the definition of that cricketing term. Perhaps he had been stationed there by John, perhaps Grattan had volunteered, or perhaps he had wandered there on his own. In any event, Grattan was there. It would normally be classified as folly bordering on recklessness, but in retrospect, it was an act of genius.

John bowled the first ball of the over, and it was a good length ball. But by now the Woodstock batter's eye was in, and he advanced down the wicket, taking a full swing, and catching the ball sweetly on the half-volley with that unique sound of willow hitting leather known to cricket lovers everywhere.

I was behind the stumps, as the wicket keeper and I saw the ball explode off the bat in Grattan's direction. There was no time to shout a warning, and even if we had, there would have been no time for Grattan to take evasive action. I saw his eyes grow bigger as the ball got closer. He didn't move, he couldn't move, and I could see the ball heading for his stomach.

My first thought was the ball had been hit with such ferocity that it would go through Grattan, and I looked beyond him to see if I could pick up the flight of the ball, but I could see nothing. Instead, much to our horror and dismay, my teammates and I saw Grattan crumple up and fall to the ground, where he lay motionless.

We were slow to react, but as soon as we realized what had happened, we rushed to his side. There was no movement from the body. John got there first, and he gently turned Grattan over. The first thing we noticed was the serene smile on his face (I mean Grattan's face, not John's). He looked at peace. The second thing we noticed was that his hands were clutched around his solar plexus, presumably where the ball had struck him. There was no sign of the ball.

"His ribcage is moving," Barry observed. Indeed it was, and we concluded—much to our relief and contrary to our worst fears—that he was alive.

"Thank goodness I don't have to break any bad news to Norah," said John with relief, Norah being Grattan's elder sister as well as John's wife and the reigning matriarch in the O'Brien clan. Our joy at this happy outcome was only slightly exceeded by what we discovered next.

John unclasped Grattan's fingers. As he did so, we steeled ourselves as we looked for the grievous wound that we were sure would be revealed. Instead, we saw a ball, a red leather cricket ball. It took a moment for the implication to sink in. We looked at each other. John, ever the quick thinker, put our thoughts into words.

"Grattan must have caught the ball!" he exclaimed. There could be no other possible explanation for it. Whether it was pure cricketing skill, or self-defence, or luck, the fact was that Grattan had caught the ball, and the batsman was out and was now wending his way back to the pavilion, shaking his head and muttering to himself. When Grattan came fully round, we were able to tell him that he had made the catch. Certainly the catch of the match. Unquestionably the catch of the season. Perhaps the catch of the century. We took great pleasure in telling him—almost as much as he did in receiving the news. As word spread, the applause rang out from the players of both teams, and the spectators gathered around the boundary.

The game continued to its inevitable end, but Grattan strutted about with a new confidence, that of a man who has been tested in battle and not found wanting. Was it not the Duke of Wellington who said "The Battle of Waterloo was won on the playing fields of Eton"? The Stage may have lost this game, but at least Grattan had showed them our mettle. We had regained our pride. We could hold our heads high. We were ready to play again.

There is little more to add. Grattan's catch is now in the annals of Stage cricket lore. Many years later, whenever John, Barry, and I gather together to reminisce about the past, invariably one of us, with a gleam in the eye, will say, "Remember Grattan's catch?" And smiles will creep over our faces, as our minds go back to that memorable day more than 40 years ago. As if we could forget!

Postcript.

I will admit to taking a little poetic licence, even hyperbole, with this story—but John, Barry, and I have talked about it so much over the years that it has become impossible to sort out fact from mythology, and I think I am quite happy to leave it there.

12

A GOLF COMPLIMENT

My passion for golf first flared in 1960, and the reason, quite simply, was Arnold Palmer. He came to the United Kingdom to enter the British Open at St. Andrews and end a long absence of American golfers from this event. He didn't win that year, but he captivated the crowd and all sports fans with his charisma, enthusiasm, and never-say-die approach to the game. His followers became "Arnie's army," and at 16, I became his latest recruit. Since then, I have probably spent more time with Arnold Palmer, albeit separated by a television set, than with anyone but close friends and family. Once, in the late 1970s, I saw him play the Canadian Open at Glen Abbey, just a few miles from where I live. He was past his best then, of course, but to me and thousands of others he was still a special draw.

I remember that on the twelfth hole he pulled his drive from an elevated tree into a copse in the valley. Between the ball and the green, apart from the trees, was a wide creek. The ball came to rest quite near me, and I had a chance to watch the great man closely. If I had been in his situation, I would have chipped out and "taken my medicine" as golf commentators are apt to say. I wondered what Arnold would do. He reached his ball after acknowledging the crowd with a bunch of smiles, each one seemingly intended for each of us. Then he surveyed the scene quickly, took a club handed to him by his caddy, and made a couple of practice swings. There were murmurs amongst the gallery. He was going for it! To be honest, I don't remember what happened to the ball next—whether he made the green or the water—but it didn't matter. The man lived up to his legendary status. Arnold Palmer doesn't chip his way out of trouble.

As far as my own golf was concerned, I didn't learn to play until I had graduated from Manchester University. Graham and I took five lessons at Altrincham Golf Club. The club is run by the municipality and lies in a parkland setting, close to the Chester-to-Manchester railway line, with a brook running through most of it. From the road you drive down a lane—nothing like Magnolia Lane at Augusta, where the Masters is played, but pretty enough—past a hotel, to the parking lot near the clubhouse. Now, you won't find Altrincham on a list of Great Golf Courses of the World, but it is full-sized, a good challenge for most golfers and, like many municipal courses, great value for money.

The professional there taught me something about the game that I have never forgotten. I doubt that he was the original source, but I found it profound. He told me there are four components to golf. First, there is the course itself; he said that even the worst course he had ever played on had always had some redeeming scenic qualities that made it worthwhile. Second is the social aspect of the game; one can meet and play with a variety of other people, most of whom will be interesting and pleasant company, at least for a few hours. Third is the exercise; walking is an essential part of golf and a round usually takes up five miles or so. Finally, there is the game itself. The pro said that too many golfers focused only on this last aspect of golf, the game. He claimed that, as a result, their enjoyment of the game was hampered because their performance often failed to meet expectations. He told us that if we remembered the other aspects of golf as well, we would enjoy the game more. I think he was right, and I have passed on that wisdom to others many times.

During periodic trips back to the United Kingdom after I had immigrated to Canada, I played the course several times. One year, in early March, I went to the course. I hadn't booked a tee-off time and wanted to link up with another group. I was paired with a couple of "elderly gentlemen" as described to me by the pro shop. I suppose they only mentioned it because I was then in my early thirties; perhaps they thought it would bother me, but I didn't mind at all.

I made my way to the first tee, where my playing companions were already warming up. They didn't look expert golfers as I approached them and I am sure I didn't either with my half-set that I had brought over from Canada. They both had on that thick, warm, but rough-on-the-skin tweed clothing that one associates with England in early spring. We introduced ourselves. We hadn't time for a long conversation, but I gathered quickly that one was Bert, a retired Labour member of parliament with a broad Yorkshire accent and a strong affiliation with the trade union movement;

and the other was his friend George, a retired doctor who took a particular delight in reminding Bert that he was one of the proletariat now.

The first hole is not particularly difficult, a slight dogleg left. I suggested that they lead the way. George stepped onto the tee, took a couple of practice swings, made a few more waggles, and proceeded to scuff the ball 70 or 80 yards down the fairway.

"Hard luck," I said, commiserating.

"Not bad," said Bert, somewhat encouragingly. "Much better than you did last week."

Bert went through similar gyrations and hooked the ball way to the left, but short of the trees and out of bounds. Then it was my turn. As always, the first shot on the first tee is a tense event, and I was nervous. Even though I hadn't much to beat, I was anxious to put up a good show. I took my practice swing and then settled into my stance. I drew the club back slowly, started the downswing—and the next thing I saw was my ball soaring straight down the fairway, well over 200 yards away. It was a tremendous shot, much better than my average drive. Bert and George were most effusive in their praise.

"Great shot!" said Bert.

"Well done. What a way to start," said George.

The three of us headed off, relieved the opening formalities were over. Bert and George each needed another couple of shots to get up to my ball, which was about 160 yards from the flag. I pulled out a five iron. As I swung, I lifted my head and caught the ball low, but luckily it stayed straight, landing well short of the green but running on and nestling 10 feet away from the hole.

"Clever shot, keeping it out of the wind," said Bert.

"You've done it again!" exclaimed George.

I tried to tell them it was a fluke, but they would have none of it. I lined up my putt on the green. I wanted to ensure I didn't make more than a four, so I hit gently. I thought the ball was going to stop just short of the hole, but in it went. I had a birdie! I looked around, beaming at my success. Bert and George were speechless, looks of astonishment on their faces, but they clapped instead. They settled for eight or more but didn't bother to mark their scorecards, and we moved to the second hole.

This hole is a tricky par four, another dogleg, but to the right this time. To my surprise, I again drove beautifully in the fairway and my companions again said "good shot" or words to that effect, but their words were a little more subdued than the exuberant congratulations I had received on the first hole. They again scuffed and dribbled the ball from the tee. As we were walking, Bert and I chatted about golf, and I assured him I was a relative beginner. For my next shot I had to hit a fairly long iron to stand any chance of getting near the green. The ball jumped off the face of the club and landed just short of the green. Bert and George murmured their praise.

As I walked up to the green I became anxious about the expectations that were being placed on me. Chipping was not, is not, and never will be my forte. I usually skull or chunk it—but this time it was perfect. The ball rolled towards the cup, looked as if it were going to drop, but stopped six inches to the left, and I tapped in for a par.

"Bad luck it didn't go in. It looked like another birdie," remarked Bert, somewhat cheerfully. I sensed that Bert and George were getting a little self-conscious about their play. Sometimes good play by one can raise another's game, but mine seemed to deflate my companions, and I was sorry if their enjoyment of the game was not what it usually was. On the other hand, I had a birdie and a par in the first two holes and was feeling confident.

The third hole is a short par four, with a pond near the green on the left. I pulled my drive slightly and was faced with a tricky shot over the pond to the green. Bert and George clustered around me. A lovely wedge shot cleared the pond, missed a bunker by a couple of feet, and took a nice bounce to the right towards the hole. It was a truly great shot! I stood up, flushed with pride. That was enough for my friends. I turned around, ready to receive the praise from my playing partners. Bert put his hands on his hips and just stood there, shaking his head.

"Bloody hell," he said in his broad Yorkshire accent. "It's like playing with Arnold Palmer!"

And that was that. I couldn't believe my ears. I had received the biggest compliment I could wish for. I had been compared to my golfing hero! But instead of inspiring and propelling me to greater heights, it brought me down to earth, as golf is apt to do, with a bump. In short, it finished me. I was a changed golfer the rest of the day. On the next hole, I sliced the ball off the tee, ending up in the brook short of the green. Then, on my third shot, I chipped into a bunker and ended with a miserable eight. Bert and George said it was only one bad hole, and I'd soon get back to form. But I didn't. It continued for most of the round. Strangely enough, my companions' games perked up, along with their spirits, and I couldn't help getting caught up with their infectious good humour. We spent a very enjoyable morning together and finished off with a pint in the bar. Bert raised his glass in a toast.

"To three duffers" he said.

"And Arnold Palmer," I added.

13

GOING ON VACATION

I'm sitting here at a quarter to six,
With my desk almost clean and nothing to fix.
The papers have all been put into place.
Do I detect a smug smile creeping over my face
When I think of the things that may arise,
As I hit that golf ball a million miles?

I know that I have nothing to fear
As I read my book with a nice, cool beer,
Or play some squash, or tennis, or such.
Ought I to worry? Well no, not much.

For my staff will surely the challenge enjoy
Of playing around with this new-found toy
Called freedom—no interference from Chris,
And so my staff, I must tell you this:

If the atmosphere becomes inclement
Just work harder—it's staff development.
But also remember, no coup d'état,
And think of me, with my advocaat,
Of the games I've played along the way;
There's one I'll definitely not play
As I'm off from the office for some 17 days;
I'm sure you've guessed it, it's "Simon says"!

Written with tongue in cheek on August 4, 1989, before taking the family to Myrtle Beach. Norm Simon was my boss at the time, and it should be noted that advocaat is not one of my favourite drinks, but it rhymes, sort of, anyway. Poetic licence!

14

MOVING THE PIANO

"All you have to do," said Barry, "is move it, and you can have it." The "it" in question was a Wormwith upright piano, all 700 pounds of it, mostly cast iron, built in 1918 in Kingston. Our friends Barry and Valerie were moving and, because of space limitations, had decided to buy a modern keyboard instead. They offered the piano to us because they knew that I had an urge to play occasionally, belatedly trying to make up for lapsed piano lessons when, as a boy of ten, I had opted for soccer, instead. Not that I regret the choice I made at the time, but I now recognize, with the benefit of hindsight, that it would have been possible to do both.

"Thanks very much," I said, and I meant it. The piano had seen better days, but it had accompanied, quite literally, some great parties over the years, with the melodies of the day thumped out on the ivory keys. The varnish on the wood was worn, and the piano top was discoloured by the stains of countless cups and glasses containing tea and coffee, wine and beer that had been placed upon it by those gathered around to sing to the music or just to listen. The piano was destined to go in our basement, to complete the renovation I had recently proudly finished. I had built it—with pine panelling and a pine bar complete with hot and cold water and lights—by meticulously following a design I had bought. The piano would be a nice, nostalgic touch.

Ena looked through the Yellow Pages and found a small company—"Piano Movers. We Move 'Em, You Play 'Em," or something like that—for whom moving pianos was an obvious specialty. It was the first one we noticed; presumably that was why the company had picked the name it had, and there didn't seem any point in going any further. Ena is the best at negotiating, so she was the one to call.

"Piano Movers here, Sid speaking," said the voice; Ena thought the voice sounded "old."

"We need a piano picked up and delivered to our house," Ena said. "In the basement," she added, so as to ensure they were apprised of the exact scope of the task.

"No problem," Sid said, "Clive and I can manage it." A date and a time were arranged, and sure enough, fairly promptly on the appointed day and at the appointed hour, Clive and Sid arrived at our door, with the piano strapped to a dolly. Sid was the boss and, as Ena had deduced, he was well into his 60s. He was about 5 feet 6 inches tall and weighed about 130 pounds, spread on a very thin frame. Clive, on the other hand, was more than six feet, very muscular and thickset, with large biceps and neck, and looked much more like a piano mover than Sid did. If Sid was the brains of the partnership, Clive was the brawn; it couldn't have been vice versa. Picking up the piano had been a "breeze" they said. Our confidence rose.

They pulled the dolly up a couple of steps into the long hall, where it was plain sailing until they reached the end of it and had to turn left. Immediately after this turn to the left was the door opening onto the basement stairs, and opposite this was a two-piece washroom. After some attempts, including removing the basement and washroom doors, Sid determined there wasn't enough space to turn the dolly and the piano around so they could lower both down the stairs.

"What are you going to do now?" I asked worriedly. I so wanted that piano in the basement.

"We'll just have to lower it by hand," Sid said confidently. "Only this sucker is a bit heavier than usual. Clive will be at the top, lowering it, and I will be at the bottom, helping support it and guiding it down the stairs at the same time." I looked at Sid again. I was dubious.

"I'll give you a hand," I said before I could stop myself, regretting it the moment I said it, and seeing the look of alarm on Ena's face.

"First of all," Sid said, looking at Ena, "have you got any sugar?"

"Yes, of course, but what's it for?" said Ena, somewhat bemused.

"It'll give me strength," he said.

Ena and I looked at each other. *Is this for real?* we thought.

The sugar was produced, together with a spoon, and Sid, with a melodramatic flourish, swallowed two heaped tablespoons of the white granules and said, "Now I'm ready." I was glad he was, though I wasn't convinced, and I wondered if this was all part of an act to justify the fee. For her part, Ena quickly vanished upstairs, and I heard the sound of the central vacuum going shortly thereafter. I remember thinking it was a strange time to vacuum, and I only learned later that it was to take her mind off what she thought was a calamitous situation developing. If I had been smart I would have seen her actions as a warning, like a dead canary in a mine. But I wasn't and I didn't.

We slid the piano off the dolly and positioned it at the top of the stairs on its end, ready to make the descent. There was just enough room for Sid and I to take our positions on the stairs, with walls on both sides most of the way down. So far so good. We helped Clive position the rope under the piano, and he tied one end of the rope firmly around his waist, taking up the slack of the rope with his other arm. He was going to release the rope slowly with his right hand, which would lower the piano, and we were going to guide it down. The moment we got the piano to the topmost step Clive saw a problem.

"You'll have to help me support the weight because I can't hold it on my own," explained Clive. I began to wish I was anywhere but alongside Sid who, unlike me, didn't seem at all troubled by this latest turn of events. The piano began its controlled slide slowly down the stairs. It was heavy, and our job was made more difficult by the absence of anything to hold onto. The piano went down a couple of feet. The three of us were feeling the strain. I could hear Sid's heavy breathing, I could feel the weight of the piano pressing down, and I could see Clive's face as I looked by the side of the piano. The sinews and veins on his neck looked as if they were ready to burst, and I'm sure I must have looked the same to him. The piano went down another few feet, until we were about a third the way down the stairs.

Then, out of the blue, Clive shouted, "It's going!"

It took a moment for this to sink into my brain. *What does he mean? Where is what going, and when?* I thought to myself, and then I imagined what he meant. I visualized this piano, out of control, lurching down the stairs to the bottom, with Clive not far behind since he was tied to the piano, rolling over both Sid and me in the process—for there was nowhere for us to go. I felt sorry for the people that were going to have to peel us, kids-comic-like, off the stairs, and I thought, as everyone must in similar situations, that I was much too young for this to happen to me. I began to think of all the things in this life that I would miss. And I hadn't even said goodbye to Ena! But somehow, I don't know how, the piano didn't roll over us. Somehow, the three of us summoned up enough strength to prevent the piano from "going," and we continued to slide the piano down the stairs. I counted out loud the stairs one by one until we reached the bottom, where I sat down, shaking like a leaf. Sid soon recovered his composure.

"See," he said. "I knew we could do it." But he didn't fool me. We rolled the piano to its new location and I took a solemn vow there and then that never again would I volunteer to move any large piece of furniture, and particularly that piano! I paid Sid and Clive and gave them a generous tip—partly, I think, because I was so relieved that they were unhurt—and I thankfully closed the door behind them. Then I didn't reach for sugar. Out came the bottle of scotch.

A few years later, when we bought another house, I warned the moving people about the piano. "It'll take four of your best," I said, and I ensured I was out of the house when they came. The piano wouldn't go down the basement stairs at our new house. At least that was the reason they gave when I returned home. I wasn't sure that I believed them, and I felt a little miffed that they had denied themselves the experience, if not the pleasure, of taking it down the stairs. *They* had taken the easy way out.

For a while the piano cluttered our family room, and then I paid another moving outfit to partially dismantle and reassemble it in the basement. Finally the piano was where it belonged, and I looked forward to playing it again. When I did, it didn't sound right. Some keys sounded a little flat; some others sounded, well, really sharp. I thought it just needed time to acclimatize. I gave it a few weeks, but it didn't get any better. I was disappointed. Then I had a brainwave. *But of course, how silly of me! It hasn't been tuned, perhaps for a long time. That's all it needs.* The thought cheered me up.

I called up a well-known piano company to send out a piano tuner. Much to our surprise, who should come out but Robert Lowrey himself, and I smiled in anticipation of the better sound that would shortly emanate from our old piano. Robert examined the piano carefully, running his long fingers over the various component parts. He played the keys and tut-tutted a few times. He then took off his glasses, looked at us gravely, and gave us the bad news, much as a doctor would with a patient.

"Some things are old, worth saving, and can be saved," he said seriously. "Others," he went on, "are old, not worth saving, and cannot be saved, anyway. This piano is in the second category. It has been severely damaged over the years and has been reassembled incorrectly. I would be wasting my time and you would be wasting your money for me to spend any time on this. I'm sorry. I will be glad to give you a modest credit on a new piano." He had broken the news to us as gently as he could, and we thanked him for coming.

The piano stood forlornly, unplayed, in its corner for a few years, until we had the basement renovated and I had to make a decision. I didn't take long to decide. I gathered my tools around me and began dismantling the piano, piece by piece, taking each one upstairs to be put into a dumpster. I was sad as I thought of the original craftsmen building the piano nearly 100 years ago and of the innumerable parties, singalongs, and Sunday school concerts it had supported. Finally, all that was left was a large piece of cast iron weighing several hundred pounds. With assistance from our strong son, I was able to take it away for scrap.

Then, like Barry, I went out and bought a keyboard, which I can carry with one hand.

15

My Treatment of Doctors

I have always been somewhat in awe of doctors. I am not sure why. I have seen a lot of them in my time, and I have heard enough stories about doctors and the medical profession in general, some from my sister, Christine, who was a career nurse and midwife, to have debunked any lofty allusions. But there it is. It translates into my willingness to follow their instructions to the letter and to do everything I can to please them. I seem to have the philosophy that any illness I have is a reflection on how they have taken care of my body, and I feel sorry to have let them down. It's as if their care, or lack of it, somehow gets put into a report card on their performance and given to some higher being.

In my early twenties, I was hospitalized for an illness that at first confounded the doctors. I was in a teaching hospital, and my doctor asked me if I would mind being examined by a student doctor. It would be a full medical, including a rectal examination. The latter didn't seem to be as common in those days; now they are part of annual examinations, but I suppose annual examinations weren't as common, either. If you were sick you went to the doctor, or he (and it was always a he) came to you. If you weren't, you stayed away.

"Of course not. Everyone has to learn sometime," I said in my best public-spirited manner.

"Thanks very much," the doctor said. "He will be along in a minute. His name is Richard Alexander." The name sounded familiar. And so he was. I recognized him the moment I saw him. He was not as chubby as I remembered him, but I still knew him. He had attended the same school as I, only a couple of grades lower. I hadn't known him well and only with that kind of superior air with which one treats those more junior in a school. I remember him literally causing a stink when his Bunsen burner went amok in a chemistry laboratory. I am not sure he was really to blame, but his name got associated with it.

One of the things that allow us to cope with intimate examinations by doctors is the knowledge that a relationship with a doctor is professional. Their independence, objectivity, and dispassionate concern are what make the relationship work. That's why doctors don't usually treat members of their own families. That's why I felt uncomfortable about what was about to happen. I was thinking, *I don't really want Richard*—and yes, we shortened his name to Dick—*to put his hand* . . . Well, you know what I mean. But before I could take any evasive action, Richard said, "Hello, Chris, nice to see you again," and put out his hand for me to shake. I am a bit of a coward, and with my doctor present, I remained silent about my concerns and allowed the examination to proceed. In fairness, Richard conducted it very professionally.

The longevity genes on my father's side are not very good. Both my father and his father died in their fifties with heart-related conditions, and for many years my doctors have closely monitored me. I have tried my best to control my cholesterol level by diet. Despite these efforts, my doctor observed once that my level had spiked and was outside the acceptable range. He cautioned me and said that I must try even harder to get the level down or else I would have to go on medication. Like a penitent schoolboy, I said I would do my best. And I did. I went on an even more concentrated effort to restrict my intake of saturated fats, to eat foods rich in omega fats, and to exercise regularly.

Six months later, when I next saw my doctor, he pulled out the blood-analysis report from the lab, and I prepared myself for the worst.

"How is the cholesterol level?" I asked timidly. He looked at the lab report, which he had not read before. He checked again my last reading, and then he broke into a broad smile.

"The level is considerably down. You really have made an effort. Well done." I blushed at such praise. He went on. "You've made my day. You can't imagine the number of times that I tell patients to do things and they don't. I know they don't. But it is so rewarding, even once in a while, that a patient follows my advice and it has worked." He looked so pleased that I was caught up in his enthusiasm, and we both shared in the celebratory mood. We almost hugged each other. I walked out of his office feeling very satisfied that I had made my doctor happy, and the impact on my own health seemed by contrast almost irrelevant.

However, this desire to please can go to absurd lengths. Once I had a bad cough that would not clear up with the usual over-the-counter medication. I saw the doctor, and he asked me to go next door into his examination room and get ready. I wasn't quite sure what "get ready" meant, but I hadn't had the presence of mind to ask, so I decided to take off all my clothes except my underpants, just to be helpful and perhaps because I thought it might save time in the long run. So there I was, half-naked, sitting somewhat self-consciously on the edge of the examination table when he walked in. He looked at me, a little surprised. "I only meant you to loosen your shirt," he said as he took out his stethoscope.

Then there was the time when I had one of my annual examinations. The doctor had been examining my eyes with a flashlight, probing into the corners. He moved the light away and then said, "Open wide." I, being anxious to please, strained my eyelids as much as I could to make them wider. I tried as hard as I could, but quite frankly I did not know what muscles to call upon to help. But I made a valiant effort. I am sure my eyes were the widest they have ever been before or since. My doctor noticed my efforts. However, instead of thanking me for my cooperation, he merely looked at me in an amused and somewhat disdainful way and said, "I meant your mouth. Open your mouth. I am trying to look at your throat!"

A few minutes later, he was testing my reflexes. You know the routine. He took out his hammer and hit just above my elbow, which did the expected thing and jerked back. He then moved on to my legs and held the right knee while he tapped it. It too jerked back. So far so good. He moved on to the left leg. He lifted my leg and raised his hammer. But before he could strike, my leg jerked. "Hmm," my doctor said, "you really do have good reflexes. Amazing reflexes, in fact! I could write a paper about you in the *Canadian Medical Journal*." I shrunk in embarrassment. The movement of my knee was quite accidental, but it illustrates the lengths I can go to please my doctor!

16

ANNE CHORLTON

This story is a late addition to my collection. As I was editing the stories in preparation for publication, I thought of my parents, Anne and Arthur. The influence of my father on my life has been profound: the schools and university I went to; the company I first worked for; the sports I enjoyed playing; the sports teams I support to this day; Rotary; public speaking; the long illness he endured—I could go on. Many of these topics are parts of the stories in this collection. But I realized that my mother had been mentioned only peripherally, and that increasingly began to bother me. While I never intended these stories to be an autobiography—and consequently there are some people who have played prominent parts in my life who are only mentioned briefly, if at all—I felt that this collection would be incomplete, at least in my eyes, without some focus on my mother.

Anne Gatley was born in 1909, at Knutsford, in a house on King Street, one of the two main thoroughfares in the centre of this delightful market town in Cheshire. It is perhaps best known because Elizabeth Gaskell, the Victorian novelist and author of *Cranford*, lived there for many years and was buried in the cemetery of the Unitarian chapel.

My mother's birth certificate names her as Annie, after her mother, but she never liked this name, preferring to go by Anne, "with an *e*." She was an only child and always wished she had siblings. Her parents ran a series of public houses and cafes; her father, a chronic asthmatic, provided the name as landlord and kept the books, while her mother ran the businesses. From an early age, Anne helped her parents and developed a love of cooking, which she pursued through formal training at a technical college in Manchester.

She continued to work in the family businesses until the early 1930s, when she wanted more independence and the opportunity to earn some money. She applied, somewhat against her mother's wishes, for a job with the Mid-Cheshire Electricity Supply Company, as a cookery demonstrator. She was successful and travelled around the area in her own car, a little Austin 7, giving cooking demonstrations on the new electric stoves of the day, sometimes in homes, but more often at agricultural shows and country fairs. This was quite an adventurous occupation for a woman by the standards of the day. She soon acquired a professional reputation and was asked to be the judge of various culinary competitions, from bottled fruit to cakes and pies, a role she continued for many years after she was married. I remember as a boy accompanying her on some of these judging expeditions, admiring how skilfully she managed the politics and jealousies surrounding those contests, because first prize in fruit bottling or apple pie-making was eagerly sought after in rural Cheshire.

It wasn't long before she met Arthur Chorlton, an electrical engineer with the same company, who was busy with the electrification of farms and industries. I know relatively little of their courtship, which went on for some time, but her mother was reluctant to lose the services of her only child, particularly as the health of Anne's father was deteriorating (he would die before I was born in 1943). I expect plans for marriage were hastened by the darkening clouds over Europe and the prospect of war. They were married in May of 1939; my father was 35, already well established and active in the community, and my mother was 29. Placards at the wedding, a video of which still exists, describe clever puns on their electricity and soccer interests: "2 Sparks, 1 Unit" read one; "Hearts 2, United 1" read another. As part of their honeymoon, they watched the soccer cup final at Wembley Stadium in London and saw *The Taming of the Shrew* at Stratford upon Avon, both events becoming from then on part of the family folklore on how my father was orienting his new wife.

No time was wasted in starting a family. A daughter, Christine, arrived in June 1940; I came in 1943 and my brother, Graham, in 1946, and during this time Anne developed asthma herself. In the late '40s, her mother came to live with us; she was an expert cook in her own right. This provided, on the one hand, generous and willing extra help in looking after the growing family, but on the other hand created some complex situations because of her domineering personality. My father, Arthur, was active in many things: the Home Guard; Rotary; Freemasonry; his church; voluntary causes, and most evenings through the week he would be engaged in pursuing them, but weekends were for family. Anne provided loyal support wherever she could—accompanying him to functions, baking for church bazaars, entertaining colleagues—but primarily she saw her role as creating a home for the family and making everything work. She was the one who nursed us when we were sick, listened to our problems at school and, we soon learned, didn't feel it absolutely necessary to pass on everything we told her to Arthur, so that we could usually confide in her with confidence.

Anne was a terrific all-round cook, though her specialty was baking, and once a week when I came home from school the aroma of freshly baked pies and cakes would greet me as I opened the front door. When I went to school camp for the first time at 11, she baked a chocolate cake for me to take with me to share with my pals after lights were out, so I wouldn't be homesick. She thought it would last a couple of days, at least, but it was so good it only lasted one. We ate it with the aid of flashlights, to the sound of rain pelting on our canvas tents.

We were fortunate in living a very comfortable life, but this changed in 1958, when Arthur became ill. Ironically, his illness was triggered by catching a chill while watching his beloved Manchester United play at Old Trafford, Manchester, soon after the Munich crash. A series of heart attacks followed and then a stroke that impaired his speech and movement. Then, just as he was almost recovered, he was felled by a much more serious one that took away his speech, and he became semi-bedridden. These were difficult times for the family, but especially for Anne. Just as they were looking forward to easier times financially, a move to a new house, and a comfortable retirement, all plans had to be changed, as she coped with caring for a sick husband, providing guidance to three children, and running the house at the same time. But she never complained. Her cooking skills had to be honed even finer to develop ways to make meals look and taste inviting and present them with different colours and textures and the right portion size for the occasion. Her own health was in jeopardy when she developed a tumour on her spine that required a serious operation. Christine came back from her hospital nursing duties to manage the household, and Graham and I pitched in as best we could. Fortunately, Anne recovered well.

Finally, in August of 1963, Arthur had another stroke, and a few days later he died. He was 59 and she was 53, and they had been married 24 years. The last few years had taken a toll on Anne both physically and mentally, but she was very resilient and—as I reflect now, though it did not occur to me at the time—relatively young. I never asked her whether she had ever felt inclined to remarry, because she had said several times that she wouldn't.

However, I remember that not long after that she was asked to visit a former neighbour of ours who lived not far away. He was a bachelor. She went with my grandmother. They duly reported back: he was a nice, courteous man, with a very comfortable house, and they had enjoyed their visit. I thought nothing more of this event, until many years later Anne referred to it out of the blue. I remember that she picked her words carefully as she told me this man had said that he had admired her over the years and that if she needed anything she had only to ask. My mother was a master (or should that be mistress?) of understatement, and I interpreted this as her way of saying that there might have been an opportunity for marriage if she had wanted to pursue it. To my knowledge, she never saw him again.

Some happier times were ahead, as her children were married and seven grandchildren came onto the scene. She moved, with her mother, to a bungalow in Plumley, a pleasant village three miles from Knutsford. It was only half an hour from Christine who, together with Michael, her husband, kept a watchful, caring eye on her. Anne's mother died in 1974, and for the first time in her life, Anne was free to please herself. By this time, Graham had moved to New Zealand (and then Australia), and I had moved to Canada, but she took these moves as opportunities to visit places she had never been before. Her seven grandchildren were very special to her, and she had a knack for cultivating a particular relationship with each one, whether it was the little stick men she drew on birthday cards, or the time she took to learn their specific interests, or the encouragement that she gave—all accompanied by unconditional love and a mischievous sense of humour. She was the perfect grannie.

Anne used her culinary skills and the gift of a pie or cake or a simple invitation to tea to make new friends, keep old friends, bridge differences, or help someone who was sick. In her later years she started a monthly recipe column in the local village, which she kept up for many years. In keeping with the style in which she lived her life, she did this anonymously, picking up recipes from Canada and elsewhere, and only when she died was her identity revealed.

We were lucky that she visited us many times in Canada, for several weeks at a time. Once when she was scheduled to come, we received a call at a friend's house on a Sunday afternoon. It was Anne. She had arrived a day earlier than we were expecting; we discovered afterwards that we had made a mistake. We rushed to the airport, hoping that nothing untoward had happened. Such an incident would have thrown the average old lady into panic. We needn't have worried. We found her quietly sitting on a seat, as cool as a cucumber. When we hadn't been there to meet her, she had played what we called the "little-old-lady trick." She asked someone if they could help her ring us up. The way she did it would have folks hovering over her, wanting to help, in no time, and she would be so appreciative. When no one had answered the phone, she'd assumed that we would be at Molly's by the pool, it being a hot summer's afternoon, and so she called there. She had even had offers to drive her out to Mississauga. Nothing really fazed her. "It's all been done before," she would say. Furthermore, even if she had felt "put out," she would never had told us.

The "little-old-lady trick" was used in places and situations that she never thought she would see and experience, but of course it wasn't a trick; it was simply how she was. She never expected anything, so she was always delighted and very grateful with what she was given, and consequently everyone was happy to give more.

Her last years were happily spent in a lovely apartment in the centre of Knutsford, close to the train station and bus terminus, where she liked to observe the comings and goings. She passed away peacefully in her sleep in 1991. The funeral of Anne ("with an e") was held just across the road from her apartment, in Knutsford Parish Church, where she had been christened, and it, in turn, was no more than a stone's throw from the house in which she had been born. Life had come full circle.

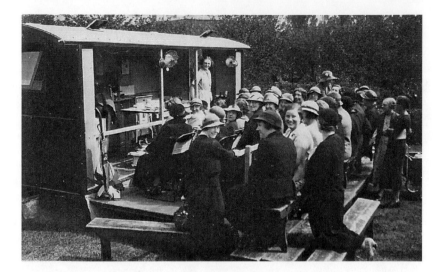

A cookery demonstration by Anne Gatley,
somewhere in Cheshire, England, mid-1930s

Anne Gatley at 21, in 1930

My sister, Christine, and Michael at the wedding
of their daughter, Jane, to Simon in 2001.

Don't they scrub up well?

17

GOOD OLD D16

In 1976, Ontario Hydro moved into 700 University Avenue, known ever since as the "glass palace." It was built by a friend of the then-premier. In its day, the building was considered an engineering marvel. The building was warmed by the heat generated from lighting and equipment, as well as humans, and it was cooled by a large reservoir of water in the basement, which also served as the emergency water supply in case of fire.

I didn't like the building. The floors were huge, 19 of them in total, excluding the basement, and the ceilings were so low that you felt you were in an underground parking garage. As has become customary, office locations were known by the floor number and the coordinates of where the office was on the floor. For example, A-1 was a corner office, which as it happens, I occupied on the top floor for a year or two in the early nineties.

Window space was at a premium and jealously coveted. Once I volunteered to move my whole department inside one of the floors, without any window space, to avoid the inevitable bickering that took place, and then my staff were all annoyed at me—but at least not at each other. Another time I moved my own office off the window in an attempt to set an example. In time I realized that the best approach was to establish a team of staff to develop the floor plan and take care of the details. In that way, all staff felt they had input into the plan

There were no doors on the offices, with the exception of the 15 most senior officials of the company, who had private offices as before. Some measure of privacy was obtained by the strategic positioning of coloured screens and plants on a hideous, bright green shag carpet. Most of the screens and carpet were still there when I left. I found it ironic that we spent billions of dollars trying, sometimes in vain, to maintain our generating stations so they would last a lifetime, but that horrible shag carpet, which was universally detested and which we hoped would wear out, seemed to be indestructible, no matter what was done to it. Indeed, the colour became more vivid as the years rolled by, as if to spite us.

The theory was that this open office concept was much more flexible for re-sorting space. One wouldn't have to knock down walls to create new space. One would merely have to rearrange the screens and plants. In practice, it didn't work quite that way; one had to wait many months for a major move. To avoid major disruptions to work and to accommodate the very specific and sensitive requirements of computers, these were scheduled at night and on weekends, when costly overtime rates came into effect.

I wrote the following on June 22, 1990, on hearing that a small office move of mine, required because of a reorganization that I had helped facilitate, was being delayed yet again. I was a little frustrated because the temporary "cell" I occupied made it impossible to hold planning meetings or confidential conversations with my staff.

> I used to have an office upon the nineteenth floor;
> It wasn't much to look, it didn't have a door.
> The light was dim, the plant was withered,
> A gloomy place, all things considered.
> And yet, with imagination, I could try
> To swing a three iron from a bad lie.
>
> I could stand upon my desk
> And gaze on all that I possessed.
> From there I could see that wondrous cave
> Where Norm would prowl and rant and rave,
> Fed paper by the mighty Helen,
> Who guards by day that communications den.
>
> And when by my office they would stop,
> I could play at traffic cop,
> And when fancy took me I could flee
> From the floor so no one could see.
> I'd creep along that one short corridor
> To freedom—oh how my heart would soar!

"I'll move to accommodate Rick," I said;
"It's only a week or two," they said.
"A fancy office and a window, too,
Only the best is good for you!"
And now, as I languish in my cell,
I'm tempted to scream and shout and yell.

How true it is that we never know
The worth of things until they go.
For now when I reflect at night
Of things that might not and of things that might,
And on my career and where it's been,
There's a place in my heart for D-16.

I sent this to the head of the space-planning department. Action was swift. Two days later I moved into my new office.

18

PLAYING HAPPY FAMILIES, RELATIVELY SPEAKING

Ena's brother, Brian, immigrated to Canada a year or two before I did and married Geraldine (Geri), a French-Canadian girl from the Gaspé, in December of 1969. I attended their wedding, much to the envy of Ena, who was in Scotland and did not return to Canada until June the following year. Being immigrants, Ena and I didn't have any family in Canada, with the exception of Brian and Geri, and for many years we celebrated Christmas and birthdays together, taking turns about. Now that we each have extended families, we pick a date in the Christmas season and those that can, come. Their children, Cheryl Ann and Michelle, are comparable in age to our own children, Lisa and Martin, and the four of them had a lot of fun together growing up. Martin, of course, was the token male and was destined to play subordinate parts, like the boss, if the girls played secretary; or the patient, if the girls played doctor; or the stage manager, if the girls wanted to dance.

It wasn't just the children who had fun. Whenever we got together, either as adults only or with all eight of us, we would play a game like charades, a word game, Trivial Pursuit, a murder mystery, scavenger hunt, or have a fancy dress party. You name it, we played it. If there was a new game, there would inevitably be a delay while Brian insisted on not only finding but reading and parsing the instructions thoroughly. Invariably, Geri's theatrical skills, honed on Euripidean Greek tragedies or in school classrooms, were brought to bear on our games. And for a while, Brian and I cooked a series of gourmet dinners that tantalized the palate, even if they were served late at night.

Apart from games, Brian and I also like sports, particularly soccer. His team is Glasgow Celtic, and mine, as you know, Manchester United. We enjoy our discussions about the sport, and the only problem exists when the two teams play each other or when *we* play each other. When the children were young, we had regular family picnics in Sunnybrook Park in Toronto, and Brian and I played our version of soccer. Goals were set up 20 yards apart, using poles acquired for that very purpose, and we took turns shooting at each other. We usually played for a set period, say 30 minutes, after which we cooled down with a beer. The winner, of course, was the one with the most goals. Sometimes judgments had to be applied on whether a shot was over the imaginary bar or outside the goalpost. This was never a problem, as we are both sticklers for fair play, and while competitive during the game, we either won with magnanimity or lost with grace.

But Brian and I have played many other sports together, including tennis, squash, darts, snooker, and golf. As for golf, Brian took up golf up quite late in life. In fact, I remember the date exactly. It was November 8, on his 50th birthday, a memorable occasion when he received his first set of golf clubs. Geri thought that Brian would like golf as a game he could play for years. Brian didn't think much of golf. Golf was a game for "old fellers." So, the candles on his cake were blown out, and some gifts appeared to mark the occasion. But when Geri presented him with a brand new set of golf clubs, he frowned.

"Who are these for?" he growled in shock and disappointment. "Take them away. I don't want them," he continued with a stronger Scottish burr than usual. Geri took it her usual good humour and resisted the temptation (perhaps it was not in her mind, but possibly it was creeping into the minds of some observers, that had they been in her shoes . . .) to wrap the clubs round his neck, tightly.

It's possible Brian thought this was Geri's revenge for buying a bicycle for her not long before. Geri had never ridden, successfully that is, a bike in her life. Brian thought it was time she learned to ride, and it would help keep her fit, as well, so his thinking went. Brian never could quite grasp the reality that Geri's sport was shopping. Geri was happy for Brian to play his sports, whatever they were, as long as she was allowed to play hers, with a comparable amount of time and money spent by her on her sport as by him on his.

I am not sure when Brian first swung the clubs, but I was certainly part of his initial forays into the game—one of the hardest games to play even poorly, let alone master. But he brought to it the same dogged Scottish determination that he brought to everything else, and he rapidly improved, becoming a competent golfer. More importantly, he enjoyed the game and grew to appreciate its subtler pleasures. Some years later, while playing in a police officers' tournament after he had retired from the force, Brian won a Cadillac with a hole-in-one at a sponsored hole. Now I call that lucky!

Luck is a funny thing. Some folks think they are lucky. Some don't. Generally, I've thought of myself as quite lucky. I have won a few raffles, nothing big mind you, but at least a couple of times I have been expecting my name to be announced as the winner just before it actually was. My biggest win was $1,000, from a draw at a restaurant in Toronto. We put it towards our daughter's wedding; it likely paid for the serviettes. But this couldn't compare to Brian's win. The only hole-in-one in his life, and it happens to be when a Cadillac is the prize! The funny thing is that Brian doesn't think he was lucky. Oh no! He says he won the car through skill, not luck. After all, as an experienced golfer, he was aiming for the ball to go into the hole, wasn't he? Fair enough. But I say he *was* lucky. He was lucky to be playing golf at all. He wouldn't have been if Geri hadn't bought him golf clubs for his fiftieth birthday!

Our penchant for games and theatrics also provided a process to solve a family dispute, in what has become known as "the trial at Myrtle Beach." Many years ago, we all went to the "Grand Strand" for a week's vacation. Soon after we arrived, we were strolling along the front, getting the feel of the place, the ladies taking the opportunity to browse through some shops. In one shop, a stuffed animal caught the eye of Michelle, who was 11 at the time. She was immediately taken with it and wanted to buy it from her allowance that she had saved for the vacation. The cost of the animal was $18, about half of her savings. She consulted her parents. Their first reaction was that it was too expensive for Michelle to buy, particularly as this was the first day of the vacation. What if Michelle saw something later on that she wanted more but didn't have any money left to pay for it? They seemed good points at the time, but Michelle could not be convinced or persuaded. She summarized her arguments, that she really wanted the stuffed animal; that it was her money to do with as she pleased; and that she quite understood that when her allowance was gone there would be no more money. Michelle was adamant.

Heated discussions took place between Michelle and her parents. Nothing could be resolved. Finally, Michelle said, "Why should you guys have the final word? I may only be 11 years old, but I have rights. I want an independent hearing of my case."

This was an intriguing idea and seemed to Brian and Geri a good way of getting out of a situation that could interfere with the vacation for all of us. Moreover, a hearing was bound to support their point of view, they thought. Besides, given our fondness for play acting, we might have some fun with it—a game where the rules were flexible, or at least open to interpretation, and the outcome uncertain. But this was serious business to Michelle.

"Michelle, we accept that you should have an impartial hearing. Both sides must agree to accept the decision. But who should act as the judge?" Brian said.

Michelle thought for a moment. She looked briefly at all of us, clearly weighing up the advantages and disadvantages of each. It didn't take long for her to decide. "What about Aunty Ena?" she said. She turned to Ena. "Will you do it?" she asked. Ena realized this might be the only way to end the impasse, but she was unsure she could adjudicate the issues adequately.

"Okay, I'll do it," she decided. "We will have the hearing tonight at 7:30 in my apartment, after we have eaten dinner. Both sides have the rest of the day to prepare their cases."

It was agreed that Michelle should have the benefit of advice and coaching from her mother on style and procedure and from her older sister and cousins on matters of content. They closeted themselves away to prepare.

At 7:30 sharp, in the judge's apartment, the hearing began. Ena had dressed herself in the most dignified clothing she could assemble from her vacation wardrobe and decided that a wig, in the form of a folded white towel, would add the right note of respect and decorum to the proceedings. A wooden serving spoon acted as the gavel.

No exact transcript of the hearing exists, but the principal participants were as follows:

Presiding Judge:	Her Worship, Aunty Ena
Plaintiff:	Michelle
Plaintiff's Counsel	Michelle, acting for herself and assisted by Assistant Counsels Cheryl Ann, Lisa, and Martin,
Co-defendants:	Brian and Geri
Chief Witness:	Brian, also known for using the aliases of "Dad" and "Uncle Brian"

I cannot recall being asked to carry out any useful office or purpose. However, it has long been my experience that I am uniquely well-equipped to carry out assignments of this nature and consequently did not feel it appropriate or necessary to bring the oversight to anyone's attention.

At the outset, the judged reminded the plaintiff and the defendant of their obligation to abide by her ruling. She also, hearing the sound of a corkscrew opening a bottle, banned the use of alcoholic beverages in the courtroom for the duration of the hearing. Soft drinks were permitted. The first round was won by Michelle.

I can report that the opening statements by the plaintiff and the defendant merely went over old ground, but the cross-examination of Brian by Michelle was illuminating, and I thought it might be crucial in determining the case's outcome.

"Would you agree that there is nothing illegal about the purchase of the stuffed animal?" asked Michelle.

"That's not the point," said Brian.

"Please just answer the questions *yes* or *no*," Michelle politely reminded the witness, with one eye on the judge. Her coaching was paying off already. "Is the purchase legal?" she repeated.

"Yes," said Brian, with emphasis.

"Do I like stuffed animals?"

"Yes."

"So it's not a passing fancy of mine, is it?"

"No."

"Is it my money?"

"Yes."

"Is it going to harm anyone else if I buy it?"

"No."

"If the money had been in my pocket, I could have gone ahead and bought it anyway, couldn't I?" Michelle was going for the jugular.

"Yes," admitted Brian.

"You were just acting as my banker, weren't you?"

"Yes," said Brian glumly.

"No more questions, Aunty Ena—I mean, Your Honour."

Soon, the judge adjourned the proceedings and withdrew to her chambers to consider the case. In the courtroom itself, Michelle was warmly congratulated by all on her professional demeanour.

Ena—I mean the judge—was out 20 minutes, long enough for Michelle and her assistants to have a game of crazy eights, though one could tell their minds were really on the upcoming verdict.

At 8:30, the door to the judge's chambers opened. The judge reappeared and took her place again at the table. She was straight-faced, giving no clues as to which side she was favouring.

"Quiet in the court," she said, banging her gavel, the crazy eights game having disintegrated into good-natured banter about whose turn it was next. We all paid attention.

"I have listened carefully to the arguments in the case, and I have weighed the considerations of both parties. On the one hand, Michelle wants to buy this stuffed animal with her own money. On the other hand, Michelle is a minor and her parents, particularly her father, want to protect her financial interests by preventing her from making what they consider to be a frivolous purchase," she said gravely. "I think it important to find some middle ground that recognizes the legitimate rights of each party."

"Someone mention a party?" piped up Cheryl. The judge frowned at her.

"Accordingly, it is my considered opinion that Michelle should be allowed to purchase the stuffed animal, on the condition that she waits at least 72 hours before making the purchase. This will give her the opportunity of rethinking the purchase. If she is still keen to buy at the end of the period, I think the parents have to recognize that it represents something important to her. And that is my decision. Are there any questions on my ruling?"

"No, Aunty Ena—I mean, Judge," said Michelle.

"No, Your Honour," chorused Brian and Geri.

"And thank you," said Michelle, feeling vindicated.

"Thank you, Your Honour," said Brian, also feeling vindicated.

"The court is adjourned!" said the judge, banging her gavel for the last time, smiling as she did so. It looked like a win/win situation for Aunty Ena!

The court in session. Ena as judge, with Michelle,
Brian, Geri, Cheryl Anne, Martin, and Lisa

A Victorian dinner party with Brian, Anne, Ena,
and Geri, with Michelle as the maid

19

REORGANIZATION:

DON'T LET IT GET YOU DOWN

In 1992, Ontario Hydro—one of the most respected utilities in the world and an important player in supporting the economic development of Ontario by bringing low-cost power to the province's growing industries, towns, villages, and farms—was in a state of crisis.

Factors contributing to this were both economic and structural. Sales had declined for several years, and the price of electricity had increased rapidly and was expected to continue. The situation was exacerbated by a leadership vacuum since the recent departures of the chairman and the president.

After an extensive courtship, Premier Bob Rae appointed Maurice Strong, the charismatic international businessman-environmentalist as chairman. Strong took swift action to address the crisis. He froze electricity prices for the rest of the decade and initiated a major cost-reduction program that would slash staff levels by about 8,000 to 24,000.

For the staff, a period of extreme anguish followed. Senior staff positions were cut by a third, and we had to apply for positions in the "new" Hydro. I was one of the lucky ones; I was appointed to head up the executive office to work closely with Strong. Those that were not selected for jobs could either take early retirement, if eligible, or take a "voluntary" severance package (VSP).

At the professional and unionized levels, staff had to be "posted" to the new organization by a complicated process involving the unions; this was based on criteria, the most prominent of which was years of service. Unfortunately, this meant that many of the bright young men and women who had been recruited in recent years had to leave.

In the context of corporate survival, all this made good sense, and it must be said that the packages were generous. But to a company and its people who had not been faced with such massive change before, where a job at Ontario Hydro had been considered a career for life, the impact on many individuals was overwhelming. The reorganization was the main topic of conversation and affected workers' behaviour on the job.

After working my own way through the process, I composed the following poem in early 1993 and distributed it to the more than 100 staff for which I was responsible, in an attempt to help them put into perspective what was happening.

This turned out to be the first of several major reorganizations affecting Ontario Hydro and its successor companies.

Some things make us worry,
Some things make us frown;
As for reorganization,
Don't let it get you down.

I know we need to mend our ways,
I know we need to change;
But how often do you have to tell us?
I'm tired of that refrain.

Am I a receiving location?
Or am I one that sends?
What a drawn-out process!
Soon I hope it ends.

Am I with the old Hydro?
Or am I with the new?
Will I be one who's asked to go?
Or will I be one of the few?

Will I take early retirement?
Will I take VSP?
Does anybody really care
What happens to me?

Will all the jobs get posted?
With my friends do I have to compete?
If I help them in the meantime,
Will they do the same for me?

And yet when I think of my life
And what there is left to do,
Is today really relevant
To the future of me, or you?

Some things make us worry,
Some things make us frown;
As for reorganization,
Don't let it get you down.

20

The Best Caesar Salad

"What's a recipe doing in this collection of stories?" I can hear you saying. Ah well, this is not just a recipe. A whole personal social history can be written about this salad and the part it has played in my life. In fact, I can imagine, when that dark day comes, as inevitably it will, and I pass from the face of this earth, there will be some who will forgive and forget my odd transgressions, or discount and ignore my minor triumphs and successes, and will focus instead on that one attribute of mine that made a real difference to them and their lives.

"Oh," they will say, smacking their lips, "he could make a good Caesar salad. I will miss those." What an epitaph!

The recipe is originally based on one given to me more than 30 years ago by my friend Tony, who is no longer with us. It evokes memories of steaks sizzling and of sunsets glittering over the Kawartha Lakes. Since then, I have refined it to reflect my own taste and the influence of others I have eaten (other salads, I mean, of course).

I have made the salad for family and friends. It has been served at bridge parties, pot luck suppers, Rotary barbecues, office gatherings, and various celebrations covering Christmas, Easter, Thanksgiving, births and birthdays, engagements and marriages—though not, as far as I can recall, at a funeral. I can't account for why it has not been served at a funeral, but I'm confident that sometime that gap in its resumé will be filled.

Whenever we are invited somewhere, Ena often asks, as one does, "Is there anything we can bring?" Sometimes, they will request a salad. But, interestingly enough, they often don't just say "bring a salad"; they say "bring one of Chris's salads," much to Ena's delight, as she can then turn the task over to me.

No one has told me that they don't like the salad, and most compliment me in such glowing terms as would be normally accorded a heart-transplant surgeon. The one exception occurred when I was in England, and some friends who had heard reports from my family about my salad asked me to make one for a party they were having. They wanted it just the way I make it, "except," they said, "we aren't very keen on garlic or anchovies, so could you make it without?" I assured them that it wouldn't really be a Caesar salad without those ingredients, but they persisted, and I, not anxious to create a fuss, acquiesced. The resulting salad dressing, of course, didn't taste anything like it should, which would have been quite acceptable to me—except that my friends continued to promote the salad as "Chris's famous Caesar salad . . . from Canada," as if to authenticate it.

I imagined everyone muttering to themselves, "This doesn't taste anything like a Caesar salad," and so I had to mount a counterintelligence offensive, whereby I went round telling everybody that I had been asked to omit the garlic and anchovies. But this happened in my early days as a salad maker. Now, to protect my integrity, I don't permit any intrusions or instructions. It is my way or not at all.

The recipe has been communicated in almost every way known to man. I have passed it on verbally and by telephone and fax machine. It has been written down and typed. It has been photocopied and photographed, and it has been sent by regular mail and e-mail. I have been watched making it, and I have been videoed making it. I said *almost* every way known to man because, to the best of my knowledge, it has not been transmitted by jungle telegraph or smoke signals. That doesn't necessarily mean that these methods have not been used, merely that I am unaware of their use. Notwithstanding all these efforts to communicate the recipe, people often tell me that they have been unable to replicate it.

"Did you use all the ingredients?" I usually ask when this happens.

"Well, I didn't have such-and-such a thing, so I substituted this or omitted that," is the reply as often as not.

"It shouldn't be surprising, then, that it doesn't taste the same," is my retort, with a superior air.

So, finally, here is the recipe. But remember you can follow the recipe and still not make a successful salad. To achieve perfection you must be bold. It is not for the timid.

Croutons

Homemade croutons are essential. Nothing bought can come close to them in taste and texture. Use some old bread, like a kaiser or some Italian bread; crusty is good. Sliced bread will work if nothing else is available. One kaiser does enough croutons for at least four people.

Cut the bread into one-inch cubes and place in a bowl. Drizzle with one tablespoon of olive oil and toss. Put the croutons on a baking sheet. Sprinkle with chopped garlic or garlic powder (I use the latter). Toast under grill for a few minutes till nice and brown. Turn cubes, and toast again till done. Croutons will keep for a couple of days or so and can be done ahead of time. Croutons are delicious by themselves and are liable to be eaten by passersby. To help prevent this, I usually count the croutons and announce the total to anyone in the house, so they know I am watching.

Salad Dressing

About 1/3 cup of olive oil (other vegetable oils will work, but olive oil is really best)

1/4 tsp of freshly ground black pepper

Salt, as required (I skip it, since the anchovy paste and Parmesan cheese have salt)

1 tsp of dry mustard

1 tbsp of cider vinegar (I actually use slightly less)

I tbsp of lemon juice (I actually use slightly less)

About 4" of anchovy paste (This comes in a tube. It can be located in the refrigerated part of the supermarket, with cheeses, etc. Store at home in the fridge. This is an important ingredient, even if some folks don't like anchovies on their pizza. Anchovy fillets can be used, instead.)

Several dashes of Worcestershire sauce

A couple of dashes of Tabasco sauce

2 cloves of garlic, minced or finely chopped (can be a bit less or more depending on taste)

About 2 heaped tbsp of light mayonnaise. The old recipes used to use raw egg yolks, but light mayonnaise is better and healthier

About 1/3 cup grated Parmesan cheese (Grating your own is best, but bought grated is fine)

One romaine lettuce, washed and well-dried and torn (not cut) into small pieces, refrigerated until used.

Preparation

I don't prepare the salad at the table, as they do in many restaurants.

I use a plastic container to mix the ingredients for the dressing. Alternately, it can be mixed in a food processor. Mix salt (if using), pepper, vinegar, and lemon juice with mustard. Add garlic, anchovy paste, Worcestershire sauce, Tabasco, and mix well. Add oil and mix again. The dressing can be made ahead of time, if required, and stored in the fridge. It will get stronger the longer it is left.

Just before serving, add the mayonnaise and mix really well. My little coffee whisker comes in handy here.

Put the shredded lettuce in a salad bowl. A wooden bowl is traditional, but I prefer a glass one. Sprinkle the Parmesan cheese on top. Add the salad dressing, and toss well. If the salad dressing seems a little dry, you can always add more olive oil.

Add croutons, toss again, and serve immediately on plates, not bowls. Have freshly ground pepper available.

Serves 4 to 6 people.

21

THE COST OF A HAIRCUT

The age at which one becomes a senior has become blurred in recent years. With this seniority, of course, comes the availability of discounts on the purchase of a wide range of items. The discounts most obvious to me as I was growing up were those for bus and train fares, which began at age 65. Now there are many discounts available on attaining the age of 60, and I am within a year or so of that threshold. Financially, I am looking forward to receiving these discounts, but something is bothering me. I have never heard of anyone mentioning it before, but in the interest of furthering gerontology studies, I feel obliged to raise it now. The fact is, although I want to qualify for these discounts, I don't want to look as though I am eligible for them!

It's bad enough when cashiers at the liquor store ask me if I need help carrying my purchases. Initially, I wondered if they were making not-so-subtle references to the amount of alcohol I was buying. Then I realized that it was because of the "age thing," and I became quite upset about it. This offer is often made to women, irrespective of age. But with men it is different. I have since shrugged off all such discriminatory offers of help, and now I make deliberate efforts to carry out my bottles with nonchalant ease, more nonchalant than perhaps I feel, but I want to make my point.

Even more serious issues occur when I play golf. Sometimes I play with friends who are eligible for a seniors' discount. I have adopted the approach that, as I am not 60, I will not attempt to claim the discount. When registering, I occasionally get, "You aren't a senior, are you?" which pleases me and permits me to lightheartedly reply, "No, of course not" and then to cheerfully pay the proper rate. After all, golf is a game of honour. It is interesting to note that you won't get a discount on a bus without proving you are a senior with some kind of official identification, but at a golf course you can get discounts worth many dollars based simply on your word. But golf is like that. Put the biggest scoundrel on a golf course with a couple of other players, and he is a changed man.

A few months ago I went to my local driving range and asked for a large bucket of balls. I paid the $8 as requested to the young woman behind the counter and walked out to collect the balls. Only then did I realize that I had been charged the seniors' rate. While I was $1.50 better off, I was concerned on two counts. First, it was an unwitting breach of my personal ethics to receive a discount I was not entitled to. What kind of example was I setting? If everybody took advantage of such situations, where would we be? Not only would the price of a bucket of balls go up for everybody, but it could lead to an explosion of greed in an already greedy world! Secondly, I was also concerned by the fact that I must have looked like a senior to the young woman. After all, she hadn't even queried my age!

A week later, I returned to the same driving range and again asked for a large bucket of balls. This time I was charged $9.50. On the one hand, I was pleased she didn't think I looked like a senior, but on the other, I was paying $1.50 more. I thought about saying, "You only charged me $8.00 a week ago," but remembering my personal code of ethics, I said nothing.

The next few times I found I was not being charged consistently at one price or the other, and I began to look for an explanation of it. One clue came when I had a haircut and then went straight to the driving range. I had been charged the more expensive "young rate." I thought for a moment and wondered whether the haircut might have something to do with how old I looked. While I have a good head of hair for my age, my temples and sides are somewhat grey, and the amount of grey hair increases as the hair gets longer. A haircut temporarily removes some of the grey. Could a haircut be a factor in this pricing issue? I decided to put my theory to the test. Two weeks later, with my now longer and greyer hair, I purchased a bucket of balls—and was charged the seniors' rate. My theory seemed to work! But I had to confirm it.

When I went to the driving range after my next haircut, I could feel the excitement beginning to mount as I entered the pro shop. "A large bucket of balls, please," I said to the assistant, trying to sound normal. "That will be $9.50" she replied. I wanted to jump over the counter to hug and kiss her, but I couldn't and I didn't. Neither did I shout "Eureka!" nor run naked through the streets, like good old Archimedes, although I could now appreciate how he must have felt. My theory had been proved. I thought briefly about ways of capitalizing on my amazing discovery, but then I thought again of the ethics of it.

I decided on a compromise. I would not ask for a senior discount to which I was not entitled, and if asked, I would not claim to be a senior. But if it was assumed that I was a senior, I would accept the discount, as a kind of penalty for their making that outrageous assumption. And that it is what I am practicing today. It will only work for another year, when I shall be qualified for the seniors' rate. Then I shall be able to insist on the seniors' rate even if—and I hope this will happen occasionally—they make the mistake of assuming I am younger. And so, the other day, when I was asked the cost of my haircut, I was able to reply, "$1.50 on a large bucket of balls!"

22

HAVE ANOTHER COOKIE, MR. STRONG

When Maurice Strong was appointed Chairman of Ontario Hydro, he brought an air of flamboyancy to the institution that it hadn't seen before, at least not since Sir Adam Beck, the founder of the company in 1906. His bold moves internally to restructure the company and make it more efficient and profitable were matched by external strategic changes to bring a more competitive company to the market place. The quick actions by Strong silenced, at least for a while, the company's critics and bought valuable time for him to focus on the longer term.

Soon after he arrived, Strong adopted a proposal from my staff to have a series of round tables across the province, to give him an opportunity to meet community, interest group, aboriginal, and business leaders; he wanted to hear their views and to present his vision of the new Hydro.

He had a style and experience that was ideally suited to the round tables. He knew what it was like to be poor, he had been a successful businessman and entrepreneur, he was an environmentalist, he had a foundation that supported aboriginal and energy-efficiency programs, and just before he joined Hydro he had been secretary general of the Earth Summit in Rio, in 1992. He could empathize with almost anyone.

My staff was responsible for organizing the events, suggesting invitees, and taking detailed notes. My role was to welcome those attending, set the context, and introduce Strong, who would facilitate the round-table discussion. These events proved to be very successful, and from an initial six meetings, we ended up with seventeen of them across Ontario, from Thunder Bay to Niagara, and from Ottawa to the Bruce Peninsula.

Never before had a Hydro chairman undertaken such widespread consultation in Ontario. I enjoyed being part of this process, and I got on well with Strong—most of the time, anyway. Going around the province with him gave me an opportunity to get to know him. Although very effusive with praise and congratulations when things worked well, he could have quite dramatic mood swings and become difficult to work with. He was diabetic, necessitating regular food and beverage breaks, and this might have been a contributing factor.

Once, in a hotel lobby in Thunder Bay, he berated me loudly because he had heard that the invitees for the round table to be held the following day were mostly men. We had been aware of the need for gender balance at the meetings, and we'd tried very hard to achieve it, but as I explained to him, there were practical difficulties. For example, we'd invited an aboriginal women's group to attend, and they'd informed us that they would be glad to send a representative to the meeting—but we learned at the last minute that they planned to send a man. Strong would hear none of these mitigating circumstances. But his mood passed, as I soon learned that it would, and I coped with similar outbursts, though others witnessing such behavior for the first time could find it a little disconcerting.

After the round tables, I was asked to become his chief of staff, as part of the reorganization underway, and I worked closely with him on a daily basis. Before taking up the position, I had heard that he objected to others calling him "Maurice," especially when they hadn't met him before, and I took the safe route and called him "Mr. Strong." I had some sympathy, I suppose, because I have always been a little uncomfortable with the overly casual North American approach when it comes to the use of first names. After a while, he raised the issue with me.

"Chris, I think it's time you called me Maurice."

"Thanks, Maurice," I said. "I will in private, but publicly I'll still call you Mr. Strong or Mr. Chairman." I thought that his position warranted respect, but not servility.

Maurice knew everybody. His environmental interests brought him into contact with many prominent people around the world, from different walks of life, including presidents, prime ministers, royalty, and film stars, and he held more than 30 honorary university degrees.

One day I was in his office when there was a knock on the door. It was his secretary, Phyllis. "Excuse me, Mr. Strong," Phyllis said, "But I have the Queen on the line."

Maurice looked across at me, his eyes twinkling. And then, without getting flustered or batting an eye, as most of us would, he looked across at Phyllis and said, "Which queen?" It was, in fact, Queen Juliana of the Netherlands.

People thought he hadn't much of a sense of humour. He had no time for jokes, but he appreciated little quips. A few of us were meeting in his office when news of a provincial cabinet shuffle came in. The new Minister of Energy and Environment, through whom Maurice reported to the government, was to be Bud Wildman. A discussion began about the implications of this appointment for the company. I could tell he was losing interest. I said, "Maurice, I guess this Bud's for you." He chuckled, which gave everyone else permission to laugh, relaxed the mood, and helped refocus the discussion.

I enjoyed working for Maurice, and he, in return, was very supportive and appreciative of my efforts, although it could be difficult coping with his occasional outburst. There was only one occasion when it nearly got the better of me. That particular morning, Phyllis came to my desk.

"Mr. Strong wants to see you," she said. "I think he's upset about something," she warned me. I went into his office, and he shut the door, confirming that Phyllis was right. I had a good relationship with Phyllis and advance warnings like these were valuable to me. Usually Maurice sat at his desk and I sat opposite. This time we sat down at his conference table. Something was definitely wrong.

"Chris, I was very disappointed to find out the other day . . ." he began, and he proceeded to go on at great length about an incident that I had failed to prevent from happening. I totally forget what particular incident he was talking about at the time, but I remember quite distinctly that it was something over which I had no control whatsoever, and that it was, in any event, something that could not—by any stretch of the imagination—be considered significant. Otherwise I would have remembered it.

"Maurice, I can assure you that—" I tried to explain.

"Chris, it's your job to anticipate these things. I rely on you to do that," he declared. I knew I should have just stopped there, but something made me go on. I thought he was being unjust, and so I proceeded to make my defence more forcefully. I should have known better. Indeed I did know better. As expected, Maurice got a little heated, and perhaps sensing he needed more energy to carry on with his criticism, he grabbed a cookie from the plate on the sideboard. He started eating it but continued talking. He began to splutter.

"Maurice, stop talking for a minute," I said. But he would have none of it. He went on and on about my (alleged) mistake. The spluttering turned into coughing. Some cookie crumbs had obviously gone down the wrong way, although many of them were expelled from his mouth in a volcano-like eruption. Again I pleaded with him. "Please, Maurice, take a breather." He ignored me and continued spluttering and coughing, with a few incoherent words gasped out in the middle of it all.

And then this terrible thought passed through my head. It seemed that all my years of training, of not panicking, of handling crises, had left me. Instead, I had this urge, an almost irresistible urge, an urge that I had never experienced before, to say something to Maurice. What I wanted to say to him, beyond anything else at that moment, was "Have another cookie, Mr. Strong." What would have happened if I had said it? Would he have choked? Could he have died? If I had said it. But I didn't. Just at the very moment when I was about to say those words and blot my spotless copybook forever, the last remnants of my training and experience must have kicked in, and instead I stood up, went to the sideboard, poured him a glass of water, and returned with it to calm him down and persuade him to stop talking. He recovered quickly. He murmured his thanks and nothing more was said.

There was never a dull moment around Maurice Strong!

23

A Humerus Story

My parents feared I had brittle bones when I was a boy. I broke my right leg jumping from a chair to the floor after displaying a pair of new shoes and then my right arm a few months later during innocuous play. Fortunately there was nothing wrong, and my limbs remained more or less intact for the next 50 years or so. This record was broken, along with my upper left arm, or the humerus, in Kingston. I had gone there to give a couple of lectures about business ethics to some fourth-year marketing students. This provided a welcome respite from the day-to-day pressures of corporate life, and the sessions went well. The professor who had asked me to give the lecture had invited me to join her and her husband for dinner, and I was looking forward to a pleasant evening.

Back at my hotel, I decided to have a bath. Just as I was reclining into the suds, I heard the telephone ring in the bedroom. I debated whether to answer it or not but decided it might be important, since only a few people knew I was there. I clambered out of the bath and gingerly walked to the bedroom. The telephone call was from a colleague at Hydro One, but it wasn't particularly urgent, only an update on developments at work that day. After a few minutes we ended the conversation. By this time I was a little cold, and consequently I hurried into the bathroom to get back to the warm waters.

My first step on the tiled floor was into a puddle I had created when getting out of the bath, and before I could do anything about it, my feet slipped from beneath, and I fell backwards. Instinctively, I put out both my elbows to cushion my fall, but my left elbow took the brunt of the impact. For a moment I thought I was just shaken, and I tried to raise myself up. The left arm gave way and flopped about in a most peculiar manner, and I knew immediately that I had broken it. I also realized I needed to get help quickly, as I was feeling the effects of shock. I managed to crawl into the bedroom, to the bedside table where the telephone was. I couldn't reach the telephone receiver, but I propped myself up against the side of the bed, brought the telephone down to the floor, and called the front desk.

"How can I help you?" asked a young-sounding voice.

"I fell in the bathroom and have broken my arm," I said. "Could you call an ambulance, because I can't make it to the hospital on my own."

"I'll call one right away," said the voice.

A few minutes went by, and then there was a knock at the door. *That was quick*, I thought, because I hadn't heard them climb the stairs.

"Come in," I shouted. The door opened gradually, and I saw a woman, probably in her early twenties, peer around the door. Her eyes widened as she saw my pose on the floor. I had managed by this time to pull a blanket from the bed to partially cover myself, although it was primarily for reasons of warmth, not modesty, that I had done so.

"The ambulance will be here shortly," she said and closed the door. She probably should have stayed with me, given my condition, but at the time I thought nothing of it. The ambulance arrived soon afterwards, and two skilled paramedics quickly took charge. I was strapped onto a stretcher, carried down the stairs, and taken to Kingston Hospital, a few minutes away. I remembered to ask them to notify the desk clerk at the hotel that I was expecting to be picked up by the professor and asked her to explain what had happened.

At the hospital I was X-rayed, had the usual battery of tests, and had a plaster cast put on my arm and shoulder. I called home to tell them what had happened and let them know that I would be staying in hospital overnight. The professor came to see me in emergency, full of commiserations and feeling somehow partly responsible. I assured her I would be fine.

The following day, Ena and Martin came to take me home. On the way we called in at the hotel to pick up my things, where they informed us that, as a generous act of compassion on behalf of the hotel management, I would not be charged for the night I had spent in hospital!

It was a relief to get home. However, over the next couple of days, which happened to be a weekend, I could tell that my arm was not immobilized; it would get into some very painful positions, especially while I was sleeping.

On Monday morning, my doctor referred me immediately to an orthopaedic surgeon, who took another X-ray. I knew something wasn't quite right when I heard him laughing as he was studying it. I couldn't see what was funny, but I was prepared to be informed, so I could share in the joke.

"You could have this cast on for a million years, and it wouldn't close this gap," he said, pointing to the X-ray, where I could see quite clearly the space between two pieces of bone. "I'll have to insert a plate to bind the two pieces together," he said. "I'll try to fit you in tomorrow after my other patients."

"Could you make the plate a little longer, so that I could keep my left arm straight?" I asked. "That would really improve my golf game."

"It's an interesting idea" he said, pondering for a moment, "but I don't think your hospital insurance will cover it."

The next morning I duly reported to the hospital and, after registration and other mandatory tests, was escorted to my semi-private room. An elderly man, whose name I later gathered was Goddard, was snoring loudly in the bed nearest the door, so I took the one by the window. I settled into the bed and began reading the book that I had brought with me, a biography of Arnold Palmer. The surgeon had said I was his last patient for the day, so I knew that there would be a wait. In time I had my pre-op medication, as did my companion, who was having a hip replacement and continued to sleep most of the day. Aside from the inevitable worrying about the operation, I found the time passed by pleasantly enough. After a couple of hours, the telephone rang by my bed. I answered it.

"Is Graham there?"

"You've got the wrong number," I said helpfully. A few minutes later it rang again. It sounded like the same man as before, but I wasn't sure. "You've got the wrong number," I said again.

As the day wore on, I began to wonder if the surgeon might be too tired to do a good job on me. After all, he would have been operating since early morning, and I didn't want him to make a mistake because of fatigue. A mental error I make when I am tired wouldn't harm a flea, but when it's a surgeon, especially my surgeon . . . well, you know what I mean. Eventually my turn came, and I was taken down to the operating theatre. I had to admit that my surgeon looked fresh enough, but the thought that he might not be bothered me. I addressed the issue as subtly as I could.

"You must be tired, operating all day," I ventured.

"Oh no, not at all. This is fun," he said and then, guessing my motive, he said, "Are you worried I'll make a mistake? Just lie back and relax. We'll have this arm fixed up in no time," he said, patting my right arm as he did so. I was about to say indignantly, "It's my left!" when he laughed, and I realized he was joking. He couldn't really mistake my arm, because the plaster was still on it.

Next thing I knew I was back in my hospital bed. The cast had gone and my arm was now strapped up and in a sling. It felt quite comfortable. The man beside me was coming round. The telephone rang.

"Is Graham there?" *Here we go again*, I thought. I had to lean across the bed to pick up the phone with my right hand. I replied that they had the wrong number. And soon there were another couple of calls asking for Graham. To each caller I gave my now well-rehearsed answer; I was getting more impatient with each successive call. On the next call, the voice explained that she was trying to reach her grandfather, who was in room 318. "But that's my room," I said indignantly. "You must have the wrong room."

Meanwhile, the nurse had come in to check on Mr. Goddard as well as me. Mr. Goddard was in some discomfort, and I realized that he was very hard of hearing. This was not difficult to deduce. The conversations between him and the nurse became louder and more repetitive, and I gathered that his hearing aids had been removed before the operation.

The telephone rang again. Reluctantly, I picked it up. "Could I speak to Graham Goddard, please?" the woman said. It was the same voice as last time. I repeated my answer. "I am sure you have the wrong number."

"He's in the next bed to you, and I'm his granddaughter!" the woman said, raising her voice.

Only then did it dawn on me. Nobody had told me that my telephone was a shared line. The incoming callers had been trying to contact the man in the next bed. Mr. Goddard and Graham were one and the same man! I was overcome with guilt for having deprived this poor old man from contact with his family. I decided to make amends. This woman was going to speak to her grandfather.

"I'm very sorry," I said trying to sounding as repentant as I truly was. "I'll get him for you. Hold on, please." I leaned over towards his bed. "Graham," I said loudly, "there's a telephone call for you." No reply. I raised my voice even more, although I was careful to keep my hand over the mouthpiece of the telephone. At the third attempt, I got his attention. I waved the phone at him, indicating the call. Then I realized. *How is he going to answer it?* Although he had a phone by his bed, I knew he was unable to sit up to pick it up. He couldn't get out of bed, and I was strapped to an IV as well.

There was nothing else for it, I thought, deciding to make a supreme effort. I moved my legs sideways and gingerly lowered my feet onto the floor. I grasped my IV pole and navigated round my bed, my left arm tight in the sling, before approaching the other bed. For a moment the wheels of my IV caught up with the bedpost, and I thought it was all going to topple over, taking me with it. Somehow I retained my balance, and I continued, although by now I was thinking this was all rather foolhardy. I arrived at Graham's bed, and I bent to lift him to a more comfortable position to take the phone. Then I retraced my steps back to my bed. I heard another of those repetitive conversations taking place, while I tried to continue with my book. Mr. Goddard didn't seem to realize that it was not necessary for him to talk loudly.

Finally, I was conscious of some goodbyes being said and repeated several times, and I realized the conversation was coming to an end. *Now, perhaps I can get some peace*, I thought, settling into the pillows. Next thing, I heard a loud noise. I looked up and saw Graham waving the phone at me.

"Can't reach to put it back," he said. "Can you help?" I almost pressed the buzzer to call a nurse, but it didn't seem the right thing to do. They might think it was an emergency. And I still hadn't absolved myself from all the guilt I felt. So, foolishly but gallantly, I climbed out of bed and made the same trek as I had before. This time I felt a little stronger and more aware of the obstacles in my path, but I told myself that it was a dumb thing to do, risking my life and limb to facilitate a telephone call. I reached Graham, took the receiver from him, and put it back.

Back in bed, I reflected on the situation. What was I going to do if the phone rang again? If it was for Graham, what could I do? I couldn't just hang up. I couldn't say it was a wrong number, since they now knew it wasn't. But I wasn't going to make that trip again just for a telephone call. Getting to the washroom was a different matter. That was important. I decided I wouldn't answer the phone at all. That seemed to be the fairest answer, as well.

I ignored the phone when it rang the next time. In fact, I never answered another call. I didn't feel particularly bad about it. Now I was finally able to get some sleep. Next thing I knew, I was being wakened roughly. It was Ena.

"Are you all right?" she asked. "I've been worried about you. I called several times, but there was no answer, so I came over right away."

"Answering the telephone is hazardous to my health," I said. And I meant it. I have the scars to prove it!

24

CATS IN MY LIFE

For 57 years I disliked cats. It is not that I would harm them or anything like that, or that I object to other people having them or getting enjoyment from them. I have just felt uncomfortable around them.

I don't know how it started. When I was growing up, we had a couple of cats at various times along the way—as well as budgies, pigs, and hens. My sister and my brother both loved cats. Once we had a cat, a very dark brown cat whose name is now rightly classified as a racially offensive term. But this was rural Cheshire in the fifties, and we didn't know any better. My brother and sister took turns to take the cat to bed with them, where they played hide and seek with it under the covers with a flashlight. As for me, I couldn't see what the fuss was all about. I kept my distance, and in time so did the cat. Eventually we had to put the cat down and that, I thought, was that.

Some 25 years later, my 7-year-old daughter, Lisa, aided and abetted by her younger brother, Martin, and encouraged subversively by Ena, asked for a cat. I resisted for a long time. I even resorted to playing the health card, because both children had severe allergies, including asthma. But they were not to be put off. Those of you who are fathers will know that there is a limit beyond which it is virtually impossible to resist any further the entreaties of a daughter (I have come to believe that this is a secret passed down from mothers to daughters).

And so I relented, not without exhorting the usual promises that they would do the feeding and cleaning. A cat was duly selected from the humane society and christened Sylvester. Even when my daughter's asthma required some visits to hospital and she was advised to give up the cat, she was adamant. Her body must learn to live with the cat, and Sylvester must stay.

I developed a cat kick—not really, I hasten to add, but simply a pretend kick that I used when I opened the door to let the cat out. My friends were intrigued by what they saw as my eccentricity. Needless to say, whenever I visited a house with a cat, it would inevitably make its way onto my lap, if only briefly, before I brushed it off, much to the amusement of everyone—which irritated me even more.

The cat even became a public embarrassment. Instead of its given name, the cat came to be called Pussy. Sometimes, when we were trying to get the cat in for the night, Ena or Lisa would stand at the open front door, shouting "Pussy, Pussy!" I mean, really!

After many years, it disappeared one day. We searched the garden, surrounding houses, and streets—and Sylvester was not to be found. Notices were quickly produced and pinned on telegraph poles. We contacted the humane society, who told us that coyotes were active in our neighbourhood, and that it was likely that Sylvester had become an entrée for one of them. The family was very upset. I, of course, was sad for them, but I was feeling for *their* loss, not mine. For a long time I thought I was free of cats.

Then Ena started mentioning that she would like another cat. The campaign went on for several months and reached its climax one Christmas, when she declared, quite literally, that all she wanted for Christmas was a cat. And so I gave in again. In the New Year, Ena and her accomplice, Lisa (now married and with two cats of her own) went again to some refuge for cats and came back with a grey-and-white cat that was named Maggie.

Even I conceded that Maggie was a beautiful cat. She settled down quickly and soon was playing games with Ena. For my part, I maintained my aloofness. After all, this was the role I had played throughout my life. And for the first couple of months, so it continued.

After an operation on a broken arm, I spent several weeks at home, and as part of my convalescence, I took afternoon naps. On waking from these, I often found Maggie curled up by my stomach or by my legs. I would quickly push her off me, only to find her coming back with something to play with, perhaps a ball of wool or some silver paper. Sometimes I woke to find Maggie perched on my good shoulder, and if she wasn't there, I would find myself wondering where she was and would search for her.

I then began to encourage her and let her stay when she came onto my lap. All of this was under cover, very top secret. The moment Ena came home from work, I reverted back to my normal self and my aloof behaviour, with respect to the cat, that is. One evening, Maggie climbed onto my lap and I petted her, thinking I was alone, but I was spotted and my cover was blown, as much to the amusement of others as my prior behaviour had been.

Once I came out of the closet, so to speak, things accelerated quickly. Soon I was feeding her treats and openly stroking her. Then I played with her, using a plastic stick with an elastic string and a feather or bell at the end it. Maggie loved to chase this around, and a ritual emerged called "play." When I sat at the kitchen table after supper, Maggie would come up to me and stretch her front paws up to my lap while sitting on the floor looking up at me. If I did not notice her, she would repeat the process often, accompanied by meows. Once I said the word "play," her eyes would light up, and if I showed signs of movement, she would bound into the hall, or the "arena" as we called it in this game, where I let her chase the ornament on the stick around and around, pausing briefly to let her catch her breath.

Maggie—or Maggs as she was known affectionately for short—was playful and well liked by visitors and friends, and I basked in all complimentary comments, as any good parent does.

Many of you will have experienced these pleasures for years and will wonder why I have made such a fuss of my experience with Maggie. I understand where you are coming from. But I have 57 years to make up.

Much to our sorrow, Maggie died when she was nine, from a kidney ailment. We have not forgotten her, but we have not replaced her. I have concluded I am a one-cat man. Every time I turn on the computer, her picture is there to remind me.

Maggie (2000–09) helping me play bridge

25

Last Day at the Office

It is December 24, 6.30 p.m. My office is quiet now. Staff have left much earlier this afternoon, trickling out unobtrusively for an early start to the Christmas holidays. The days of corporate announcements advising staff they can leave have long since gone. The Christmas music has been turned off. Even the cleaners have disappeared.

Strangely enough, I don't mind being here. This is my last day before retirement, after 32 years with the same company. The retirement reception has been held some days earlier, my family all present, with flattering speeches from the chairman and president, a voucher for a set of new golf clubs, a show of old photographs, farewells exchanged with colleagues, and emotional goodbyes to close staff. I enjoyed the event much more than I had anticipated.

But I still have some last tasks to complete. I know nothing will happen, can happen, if I don't do them, but I want to do them anyway. I finish a performance review of a promising young woman I recently recruited, and I summarize the various pay recommendations for my staff in the coming year. I write a difficult letter to a senior manager, suggesting an approach to deal with a drinking problem of one of his staff that we had discussed earlier. I respond to some last-minute e-mails. And I write a note to my successor, summarizing what I have done, to help the transition. My in-basket, both electronic and paper, is now empty.

I clean out my desk for the last time. I took most of my personal possessions earlier. All that remains are a few photographs, a paperweight painted blue, made by my daughter in grade 1, which has adorned my desk for 20 years, my diary, and some retirement gifts: a block of Stilton cheese (my favourite) given to me by an old colleague, a tin of homemade cookies given to me by a past assistant, and a Welcome sign from one of my staff from Sri Lanka. Finally, they are somehow all put into my briefcase and various Christmas bags.

I am now ready to go. But I am not anxious to go. Instead, I sit back in my chair and let my mind drift.

I think of my father, stricken by heart attack and stroke, receiving embarrassed but well-meaning senior company officials. They presented him with a gold watch to commemorate his retirement after 35 years service, a watch I no longer have since it was lost in the post somewhere between Toronto and Manchester when it was once sent for repair.

I think of my first day at work, at the same company as my father had worked, on January 1, 1964. Starting salary was about $1,500 a year. How naive I was. Midway through a degree, I had joined the company as an administrative trainee. I still recall quite vividly possessing the notion that, shortly after my arrival and after I had been welcomed and informed about my company car and expense allowance, senior executives would present me with the problems of the company, neatly summarized like a Harvard case study. They would humbly request that I take some of my time to review the material and to let them know in due course what they should do to rescue the company from the ruin that would undoubtedly ensue should I not be inclined to help them.

Instead, they asked me, politely but quite firmly, to change the towel in the men's washroom and ensure the cigarette machine was full. And after that, would I please take care of selling the tickets for tea (served by a lady who came round with a tea trolley dispensing personal advice to her customers for the various problems and ailments that plagued them). All of this required me to make a quick and major shift in attitude, and I have never forgotten this lesson in humility.

I remember subsequently undergoing an audit of the accounts for the tickets I was selling and feeling the stress of a potential error being discovered. Anyone who has experienced an audit like that knows what I mean. And now, as I am writing, I can't help but wonder if any of the recent corporate scandals might have turned out differently had senior executives been subjected to a similar experience in their early careers.

I think of Ruth, the slim telephone operator with brown hair, on whom I had my first office crush. I used to visit her late in the afternoon when I had finished my work for the day, much to the amusement of others. She was a few years older than me, and nothing came of it, except that I learned to operate the switchboard, a skill that soon became technologically obsolete. I have not thought of her for almost 40 years and am amazed I can still remember her name. I think of her as she was then, but of course, she would be almost 65 now.

I think of Peter Henderson, the mentor of my formative years when my father was incapacitated. When I told him I was going to emigrate to Canada, he wrote to me, in a letter I still have today, to say that he hoped I would always be a credit to my father. Have I? I think I have, or at least I have tried, and I take pleasure from that. I think fleetingly, but fondly and gratefully, of many other people who helped me along the way.

I think of the past year. After an unblemished sickness record, I have had two major absences. The first was an absence of six weeks to recover from a broken humerus (and no, it wasn't funny!) that happened when I climbed out of a hotel bath to answer a phone call and slipped on the wet floor on my return. The second was of similar duration, when I suffered a heart attack in my office just eight weeks before my retirement. Fortunately, I was a candidate for a successful angioplasty. I conclude that the opportunity to take an early retirement, delayed at the company's request for nine months, was serendipitous.

I remove the key to my office door and my desk from my key ring and leave them on my desk. I see that I have now only three keys, light when compared to the jailer-like set I possessed before. I gather my belongings in my arms and, taking one last look around the office, turn off the light and carefully close the door. I walk along the now-deserted corridor and through the security doors, to the elevator. It takes me down to the basement, where I climb into my car. What am I feeling? More nostalgia than sadness, with an inner peace as well, and certainly with anticipation for tomorrow. And I must remember to return my parking pass.

Illustration reprinted with permission of Torstar Syndication
Services. Only the reference to 65 is incorrect—I was only 57!

This story and illustration was published by *The Toronto Star* on December
22, 2003.

26

GOODBYE TO A FRIEND

September 28—today is my birthday. Today a close friend died. He was 57. We met as fellow immigrants from the United Kingdom who came to work for Ontario Hydro in Toronto. Tony arrived a few months before I did, and for a while we worked in the same department. We didn't have much in common. He liked puzzles and technical problems, and I liked sports and books. He was an only child, and I had two siblings. He was married, and I was single. But we got along fine. One day he asked me to dinner with his wife, Molly. She was some ten years older than he, a woman of the world and an extrovert who told outrageous stories; she possessed, in fact, some of the qualities that perhaps Tony would have liked himself. Tony was devoted to her.

They "adopted" me. I was invited to Sunday dinners, Christmas celebrations, to cottage and house-hunting excursions, and to parties. Occasionally the invitations didn't particularly interest me or were a little inconvenient. But they wouldn't take no for an answer, and I went along with much of it, although I drew the line when they initiated efforts to find me a suitable girlfriend. And it all provided a backstop to the faltering social life I created on my own.

When I got married, finding a wife without their help, they in turn adopted her, pleased at her compatibility. After Ena and I bought our first house, we stayed with Molly and Tony for two weeks before taking possession. Tony helped us move and gave me some early lessons in basic house maintenance.

In due course, Ena and I had two children, and for a while longer our lives were interwoven. And then, inevitably, as our children grew and their interests and activities consumed us as parents, we drifted apart, with only occasional get-togethers and the exchange of birthday and Christmas cards. Then they took an assignment in Africa for several years.

When they returned to Canada, they purchased a house on a beautiful lakeside property 200 miles northwest of Toronto. As our children were now grown, our paths reconnected, though not with the same frequency as before. Molly's health had deteriorated over the years due to diabetes and a variety of ailments. It was assumed that Tony would survive his now-ailing wife, and Tony took early retirement so that he could spend more time with her. Tony even administered her insulin needles.

We heard in the early spring one year that pain in Tony's back had required him to see a chiropractor. Then the pain had worsened, and he saw his doctor. Diagnosis was swift. He had inoperable cancer of the pancreas and was soon on strong pain medication. He told us the news in an e-mail.

Ena and I planned to visit them and said we would bring lunch. We decided on something light and appetizing: smoked salmon, bagels, salad, and a variety of cheeses, all of which we knew Tony loved. During the three-and-a-half-hour drive, we discussed our possible reactions to how he might look.

Tony came to meet us at the door. He had lost much weight, was obviously in great discomfort, and was yellow with jaundice. He looked worse than we'd expected, but he was clearly delighted to see us, and we shook hands. Initial conversation was a little strained. It is amazing, until you are faced with it, how difficult it is to avoid talking about the future: vacations to be taken, grandchildren, plans for the garden, and so on. But after a while things eased. We laid out lunch. Tony could only eat half a bagel, but he enjoyed our company. After lunch, we took a slow walk around the house, commenting on the low lake level. He talked about the need to train Molly on the computer while there was still time.

After a few hours we made our departure, promising to visit again soon. I hugged Molly and approached Tony. He made a move to hug me, in response to which I, a product of the stiff-upper-lip British tradition, put out my hand, and we shook. I felt a little disappointed in my own reaction and reflected on it afterwards.

Tony called later that night to say how much he had enjoyed our visit, and we resolved to go as often as we could. We returned a couple of weeks later, with the same menu for lunch. This time, he was clearly much weaker and thinner, with a voice that could only be described as a strong whisper. He had begun chemotherapy, and he did his best to amuse us with stories about his experiences and those of his fellow patients. In our walk outside, we talked about the need to bring the boat in from the water and the numerous jobs associated with the ending of summer. Mid-afternoon, we began to say the usual goodbyes. I had resolved in advance to give him that hug. However, when I approached Tony, he stuck out his hand—and again we shook.

In early September, we made what was to be our last visit. The chemotherapy had been stopped, and there was no further hope. Tony couldn't eat anything, and his system was obviously shutting down. He talked openly about the end. He was saddened that as a cancer patient he could not donate any of his organs for transplant. Eventually we had to leave, and again we made our way to the door. Tony and I looked at each other, and this time, this last, final time, we both opened out arms and hugged each other, me clutching his withered body. That was our goodbye.

He died a week later, on my birthday.

Molly and Tony relaxing at Bancroft, Ontario, circa 1995

27

A Handyman's Comeuppance

Like many men, I was never much interested in home repair jobs until I became a homeowner. Then, out of necessity because of the high cost, I decided to take the bull by the horns. So I bought one of those home repair manuals and a large tool kit on special offer from Canadian Tire—100 tools for $29.99. I knew I wasn't without some capability, because when I was 11, my mortise and tenon joint earned me second place in my carpentry class.

Over the years, through practice, trial, and error, I have learned to tackle most household repairs, with three exceptions: anything involving concrete, because of the difficulty of rectifying mistakes; roofing, because I don't like heights; and major appliances, which are too technical for me. As a result, I have acquired a variety of skills and experience, not to mention tools and manuals, from plumbing to electrical. I have derived great satisfaction from applying these skills and saving money—but perhaps more from basking in the admiration of colleagues and friends when boasting of my achievements, and lording it over others who don't even know a Robertson from a Phillips.

Ena has been very appreciative of my work, but my efforts don't come without a cost. First, I am slow—slow to get round to doing a job, slow in planning, slow in execution, and slow in completing the final 5 per cent. Compared to my work, Michelangelo's work on the Sistine Chapel over many years represents a quick paint job! Secondly, I am reluctant to ask for assistance either from friends or experts. I like to be independent. As a result, some jobs can be "pending" longer than Ena's tolerance level.

Take the sprinkler system in our garden, for example. About two years ago, one of the runs wouldn't work, an important one covering a large bed with shrubs and perennials that was difficult for Ena to reach with a hose. I opened the sprinkler control panel to inspect the terminals. Nothing seemed amiss, but I jiggled the wires on the offending terminal number five to check for loose connections. It still didn't work. And then I remembered that a few months earlier Martin and I had removed some old junipers from beneath the front window, "the ugly plants," as Ena called them. As we were digging, we'd unearthed the sprinkler system cable; perhaps we had inadvertently broken it.

It seemed that the only solution was to run another cable underground, from the programmable controller in the garage, under a concrete path, to the control panel located in the ground on the far side of the house, a distance of some 50 feet. This was too much for me to undertake. I reported my findings to Ena, who wasn't impressed and merely said, "Why don't you call in the company that installed the sprinkler system?"

I called them, but they never bothered to come, and I let the matter drop, fearful of the cost and hoping for some divine intervention to restore the water flow in the meantime. Without the sprinkler system, Ena was forced to use hoses, which are heavy and time-consuming to move, and she was not to be put off.

"Why don't you call Martti?" she asked one day.

Martti is my daughter's father-in-law. He loves nothing better than fixing things and being surrounded by parts, and the more parts there are the happier he is. Now, Martti is a fine fellow, and we get on well, but I bristled at my wife's suggestion. There was my pride to consider. And besides, I thought, what could he do? The sprinkler needed a new cable and that was the end of it.

Ena is very persistent—some would say tenacious. A week later, she made a point of discussing our sprinkler problem at an extended family gathering, much to my chagrin. She knew Martti would take the bait, and he did. He said he would be round the next day to help. Sure enough, bright and early the next morning, he appeared cheerfully on the doorstep with his tools and several devices for measuring electrical currents and suchlike draped around his shoulders or hanging from his carpenter's belt. Some people would have been impressed by this, but I thought he looked like a witch doctor.

I explained the problem to him, as well as my diagnosis and solution. I wanted to get that in first, so he couldn't take all the credit. He knelt down to examine the control panel. He checked the connections as I had and asked me to turn on the water. Nothing happened. He pulled out his instruments, which he played with for a few minutes before announcing that the wire in question was indeed dead. I smirked. This only confirmed what I already believed.

"It looks like it needs a new cable," he said.

"Yes, that's what I thought too," I said, trying to sound magnanimous. "But thanks very much for coming and checking it out. I'll just have to get the sprinkler company to lay a new cable." I made to gather up the tools, smugly anticipating the moment when we would tell Ena that Martti couldn't fix the problem and that I was right after all.

But Martti didn't leave the scene. He sat there peering at the control panel. He grabbed hold of the input cable again. He looked at the different coloured wires, and he counted them. There were black, orange, yellow, red, blue, and green, six wires in all, with green being the faulty one. Then he matched them to the terminals in the control panel.

"There isn't a match for the orange wire. There are six input wires and only five terminals," he said. He thought for a moment. "That must mean that the sixth wire, the orange one, is a spare. Perhaps if I can connect the orange wire to the terminal in question that would fix it."

I had to reluctantly agree that his logic made sense, and I silently cursed myself for not reaching the same conclusion. In a flash, Martti had stripped the orange wire and connected it to the terminal. He turned round and said, "Turn on number five." I went into the garage with mixed feelings. What would I say if it worked? I turned on run number five. Within seconds I heard the sound of water surging through the system. It was working. I thought of how I might explain to my wife. Perhaps I could pass it off as a successful joint problem-solving exercise, thereby allowing me to claim some credit. But before I could finalize my face-saving strategy, Ena came rushing around the corner, shrieking with delight. She had been in the back garden when run number five came on. She ran past me towards Martti, who was just getting to his feet. She gave him a big hug. "Martti," she said, "thank you so much for fixing the sprinkler. I knew you could do it. You are my hero!"

He just blushed and said, "It was nothing."

I agree, but his reputation is now secure for all time. I'm just not sure about mine.

An edited version of this story was published under the title "Shootout in the DIY Corral" in *The Globe and Mail* on August 8, 2011.

28

UPDATING THE WILL

We made our first will on December 28, 1975. I can't remember why it was December 28. Nothing happened that Christmas to precipitate such timing, as far as I can recall. There was no falling out at Christmas between Ena and me that would cause either of us to say, "You didn't get me what I wanted for Christmas, so I am going to change my will!" Nor did it coincide with some other life event. It may have been simply that this time was the earliest that we could get witnesses.

I know I shouldn't refer to it as "our will." It is a fact, though, that with the exception of a different name, my will and Ena's were exactly the same, comprising all of three pages double-spaced, even with all the legal wording.

The trigger to have a will in the first place was the birth of our second child. At the time, since we were both immigrants to Canada, the only relative we had there was Ena's brother, and so he was designated as being the guardian of the children should anything befall us. As the children were growing up we told them, whenever we went away, that if anything happened to us they were not to worry, because they would be taken care of by their Uncle Brian. We did this in an attempt to reassure the children, but oddly enough, despite our best intentions, it always seemed to have the opposite effect.

With the passage of time, Ena and I reminded each other that we really must update our wills. But like most people, we were busy, and we never got round to it—until just a few months earlier, when we made an appointment with a local lawyer who had been recommended to us by a friend. It wouldn't take long, we told ourselves, since our belongings and affairs generally are neither complicated nor extensive.

Once we got past the large sheepdog belonging to the receptionist that apparently guarded the premises (I mean it was the sheepdog guarding the premises, not the receptionist), the lawyer said that initially her role would be to ask a lot of questions to prompt our thinking. She opened up the discussion by asking each of us what we wanted to do with our estate (she didn't use the word *belongings*). Which child should be the executor? Did our children get on well together? What would happen if either of them predeceased us? Would we want to provide monies to their spouses, assuming no children? Suppose they were cohabiting with someone? Would it matter how long they had been cohabiting? Would there be a minimum period? Suppose there were children from this cohabitation. Did we want to recognize them? How and to what extent? Were there other bequests we wanted to make?

I don't have much experience with wills. When I was young, my father had an uncle who was married but had no children. This uncle retired with his wife to a bungalow by the sea in North Wales. Periodically we visited them, particularly during the summer, when we could also go to the beach. We took the usual little gifts one does on such occasions: a pie or a cake baked by my mother; a favourite book; and in the winter, some firewood to help light the fire. Although my father often joked about the need to look after his inheritance, he was genuinely very fond of his Uncle Ben and wrote to him often between visits.

Eventually, well into his eighties, Uncle Ben died. We continued to visit Aunty Tan much as before, "looking after the inheritance" until she died, when my mother, widowed two years earlier, was informed that Uncle Ben's will, while providing generous bequests for a number of other nephews and nieces—including some who rarely, if ever, visited him—excluded my father, apparently on the grounds that he didn't need the help that the money would represent. Aunty Tan had forgotten or was unable to change her will to take into account my mother's widowed status and worsened financial situation. I thought at the time that this was unfair, as did everybody else, but nothing was done about it.

You can imagine the discussion prompted by our lawyer's questions. Our children get on very well together, and we took great comfort that this would facilitate matters. We ploughed through the questions, and the matter of the will was done, subject to our lawyer drawing it up in legal form.

We talked about ways to designate our personal property, like jewellery, paintings, and furniture to make it easier for people to know who was getting what. Apart from making specific bequests in the will or attaching a list, there are some other good ideas for doing it as well. My mother wrote the person's name on the bottom of a piece of porcelain or furniture she wanted to give it to after her death, so that there would be no doubt. This worked beautifully when she passed on. Another technique is to actually tell people that an item is theirs when you die but that you will continue to enjoy it for as long as you live. This way, both the giver and the recipient derive considerable pleasure from the process.

After that, we said, "Thanks very much" to the lawyer and got up to go.

"Wait," she said. "Have you thought about a power of attorney in case you are incapacitated and unable to make any decisions regarding your affairs? And what about a living will, regarding your wishes in the event of impending death and the use of artificial means to keep you alive, not to mention the question of organ donations?" We looked at one another. "Yes," we agreed. "We should do these, as well."

And so we went on to the next round of questioning. The power of attorney was quite straightforward, providing we had enough confidence in the judgment of the persons to whom we were giving the authority, in our case each other and our children. I noticed the rather quaint wording in the introduction to the power of attorney: "Know all men by these presents . . ." It was very chauvinistic and almost Christmassy in tone!

The living will was more sobering. We had to discuss whether we wanted to "refuse measures of artificial life support" or "nasogastric tube feeding." This is not the pleasantest of topics to think about on a sunny fall morning when you are sipping coffee and munching on a raspberry muffin. At least the consent to donate all organs for transplant was a more positive spin on what otherwise was a gloomy part of the exercise.

We duly signed the multitude of forms (witnessed by the receptionist with the sheepdog), paid the bill, and left. The best part was still to come. I was able to tell my daughter, now 30, married, and pregnant, that she wouldn't have to go to her uncle's anymore in the event of our death. She was very relieved!

29

OUTFOXING THE SQUIRRELS

It's early winter and time to feed the birds—or, if your experience is like mine, time to feed the squirrels. Not that I feed squirrels on purpose. How many of you are faced with the problem of squirrels eating your birdseed, after you purchased it at great cost to help our feathered friends survive the winter?

Squirrels don't need help. They spend the fall collecting and burying nuts and digging up and eating the tulip bulbs I have carefully planted for spring. Birds have to live on the wing, which is why many people have birdfeeders in their garden. As a result, we get a dazzling array of birds, from the usual mourning doves, sparrows, nuthatches, juncos, and robins to the cheeky chickadees, majestic cardinals, impudent blue jays, and bullying crows.

Our birdfeeder has a steel post that fits into the same concrete hole used by the clothes dryer in the summer. It's fairly firm and secure, although not as much as it once was. Last summer I was adjusting one of the sprinkler heads located near the clothes line. The sprinkler head slipped out from my grasp, and the jet of water started pulsating towards me. Not wanting to get a cold shower, I ran backwards as fast as I could. I would have gone quite far, and certainly out of range of the sprinkler, had it not been for the fact that the clothes line post was in my way. As it was, I backed into the post at full tilt. Fortunately, the post gave way, and I went with it, sprawling on the grass. I was temporarily winded but then quickly revived by the periodic swish of the sprinkler going over my semi-prostrate form. I crawled to turn the sprinkler off and managed to get the concrete base back in the ground. I did the best I could, but now, when fully loaded, the clothes line can topple over if the wind is blowing in a certain direction.

Luckily, in winter, the frozen earth and snow provide an adequate support for the bird feeder.

We buy the birdseed at a pet store a few miles away. They sell their own brand of mixed seed (without corn, of course) for big birds, at about $18 for a 25-kilogram bag. Last time I was there, I went to the cash desk and said to the cashier—a slip of a girl of about nineteen who can only have weighed about 50 kilograms herself soaking wet—"Could I have a bag of your mixed birdseed, please?" I pointed to one of the big sacks.

"Certainly, sir," she said in a most pleasant manner. "Would you like a hand out with that?" I thought for a moment. While I usually carry out that size bag, they are heavy, and I have reached that state of maturity when I am accepting more and more such offers of assistance—and there seemed to be no good reason why I shouldn't accept this one. *Besides, it'll give one of the men a chance to show off*, I thought patronizingly.

"That would be very helpful, thank you," I said. "Perhaps there's a strong young man around who can help?"

Without batting an eyelid, the girl looked me in the eye and grinned. "Oh, we've plenty of them around, but I can manage well enough," she said. And before I could say anything else, she had moved from behind the counter to where the bags were stored. She lifted up one of the bags by a corner and expertly flipped it onto her shoulder. She turned to me.

"I'll follow you out to the car," she said, which she did quite nonchalantly before depositing the bag with a flourish into the trunk of the car, which I opened for her after a delay while I fumbled embarrassingly for the keys.

"Thanks very much," I said, feeling somewhat foolish as I climbed into the car and drove away.

And now we get to the problem with the feeder. The squirrels can climb the pole to get to the birdseed. As a result, the squirrels grow bigger before your eyes, particularly one black squirrel—fat Cyril, as I call him. Now I know there will be readers of this story who think it's unfair and not politically correct to mention Cyril's excessive corpulence. I am sorry if you feel that way, but personally I draw the line at squirrels. I think they are fair game, so to speak. Fat Cyril was a living example of why we were going through bags of seed at an alarming rate.

Strangely enough, the squirrels don't bother the birds much, who keep pecking away. Only when a crow or a blue jay swoops down from the sky do squirrel and birds alike scatter. I investigated installing a concave plastic baffle to prevent the squirrels from climbing the pole, but baffles are expensive and the pole diameter was too small to accommodate one. So I had to come up with a homemade solution. I thought of an electric fence or barbed wire, or even some jagged glass to put round the post, but I concluded that these approaches, effective though they may be, are too radical for what is essentially a simple problem. No doubt some readers facing a similar problem have developed ingenious solutions; I would be most interested in hearing about these.

I don't mind admitting that I am not without a modest track record myself in solving such problems. One morning, Ena came up to me in a hurry. "There's a skunk in the garage!" she gasped. I tried not to panic. My first thought was *What happens if it gets into the house?* and I imagined washing the house down with tomato juice, as they do with animals who have come into contact with a skunk.

"Are you sure?" I asked.

"Come and see for yourself," she said, and we went towards the garage. As we got close, she put her finger to her lips. "Shh!" she said. "It's asleep behind the door." We tiptoed the rest of the way. Sure enough, as we opened the door a little and I poked my head around, I could see the body of the skunk curled up and apparently asleep. As I gazed around the garage, I could see parts of the wall had been heavily scratched, as if it had been trying to escape. It seemed that it had been locked in the garage overnight.

We went back into the house for a conference. We didn't want to create a situation that would provoke the skunk to spray inside the garage, and we thought trying to move it with a broom would do just that. We also thought it would be better if the skunk didn't see us (not to mention vice versa). And then I had an idea. "I'm going to turn the central vacuum on," I said. Ena looked at me as though I had gone mad.

"Why on earth—" she started to say and then checked herself. She had remembered, no doubt, that the motor for it was in the garage. "Ah, you think the noise might disturb it."

"I certainly don't like to be in the garage when it is turned on," I said. "Why should a skunk?" We decided it was worth a try. We turned on the vacuum, and the familiar piercing jet-aircraft-like sound started to emanate from the motor. We looked through the window into the garage. For a minute or so, nothing happened. Then, sure enough, we saw the skunk stir from its slumber, look around as if about to complain about being awakened, and then, as if seeing there was no one to complain to, shuffle off slowly across the floor and out of the garage. We quickly closed the garage door and checked there were none of his relatives left, which there weren't.

With the memory of this success fresh in my mind, I was feeling confident I could solve the squirrel problem. What I needed was something to make the post unclimbable. A flash of inspiration came to me. What about Vaseline? I had a jar in the garage, which I used to protect nuts and bolts of garden equipment from the ravages of the weather. So I retrieved the jar and, dipping my fingers into the jar, grabbed a handful of Vaseline and proceeded to spread it liberally on the metal post. To be absolutely frank, there really isn't a very dignified way to apply the Vaseline, and I admit that this is the major disadvantage of my method, good though it is. One has to have a certain self-confidence to be able to carry it off in public. There I was, slathering the post, while my family, intrigued and curious, watched from the comfort of the kitchen, having gathered there specifically for that purpose. I saw them smirking, but I ignored them and finished the job, using several handfuls of Vaseline to completely cover the post. After washing my hands, I joined them inside.

We didn't have long to wait. Fat Cyril and a couple of his pals scampered along. Fat Cyril got to the bottom of the pole, looked up, turned his head around as if to make sure no one was watching him, and started to climb the pole in his usual way. He got a couple of feet off the ground—and my family was about to start ridiculing me—when much to their amazement and my glee, he began to slowly slip backwards. He tried to accelerate his efforts to make up for it, but he couldn't prevent himself from slipping, inexorably, back down the pole. The harder he tried the quicker his descent. When he reached the ground, he picked himself up and scrutinized his paws as if to show that he realized something different was going on, but he didn't know what.

Then, apparently undaunted, he decided to try again. This time he spurned the gradual approach and instead leaped three feet up the pole and started climbing from there. For a moment he made some progress, and I wondered whether he had outfoxed (if out-squirreled were a word, I would have used it here) me, before he slipped down to the ground as before. This time Fat Cyril didn't try again. He ran off, turning round for one last bemused look at the pole, and climbed back up a pine tree, where presumably he consoled himself with goodies from his winter store.

The Vaseline worked. My family could not believe what they had witnessed, and they congratulated me. We stayed near the window. Another squirrel tried, with the same result, and then another and another. It didn't matter whether they were grey, brown, or black, or which climbing technique they adopted. All came to the same end, even if, to put it more precisely, it was not the end they wanted. The others wondered if the Vaseline would wear off, and they kept a casual watch in the days to come. I also checked the post, but the Vaseline neither froze nor was it easily washed off by the rain. I can understand why it is used on babies. My triumph was complete.

I have thought about repackaging Vaseline and selling it at some exorbitant price as a squirrel repellent. Instead, I have decided, in the interests of science and the public good and as an example for others to follow, to release my findings to the world. Therefore, let it be known that Vaseline has been tested on squirrels and it works, even if a cousin of Fat Cyril is present in your garden. Another use for Vaseline!

An edited version of this story was published in *The Globe and Mail* on February 4, 2011.

30

LIAM'S FIRST CHRISTMAS

It was Christmas Day, 2003. Ena and I had arrived at St. Christopher's a few minutes early for the 8:30 service. The morning was perfect, just like a Christmas card, with a clear blue sky and the ground lightly covered with snow, which squeaked as we walked and formed a white canvas for our long shadows painted by the wintry sun. The church was busy but not yet crowded, and we easily found a seat some two-thirds of the way back. We left a space for our daughter, Lisa, and her 9-month-old son, Liam, our first grandchild, who we were expecting to join us, as they lived not far from us or the church. Lisa's husband, Mark, remained at home to prepare the breakfast that would await us on our return. Ena and I sat down and loosened our coats.

The church looked beautiful. There were more than the usual array of lighted candles, and a large pine Christmas tree, simply decorated with clear lights, was at one side of the altar. In front of the tree, at the bottom of the steps, was the crib. The church had been collecting the various figures in the pageant for some years, and now, as my eyes passed over the crib, I saw the Holy Family, the shepherds kneeling, the wise men carrying their gifts, and a few angels. On the other side of the altar, a folk group, specially augmented for Christmas, was playing carols in the background, carrying out last-minute adjustments to their instruments and the sound system as they did so.

I sat back in the pew, enjoying the serenity of the scene, and reflected on the past year. I thought particularly of Liam. He had been born in March. The arrival of Liam had been a joyous event, made even more so because of the difficulties surrounding his birth. His parents had been trying unsuccessfully for several years to have a baby. There had been a miscarriage or two, and Lisa had developed a condition that not only affected her own health but also complicated the prospect of getting pregnant or carrying a baby to term. We were overjoyed when she and Mark announced the pregnancy, an announcement that had been delayed until Lisa felt reasonably confident about the outcome.

But ironically, a few days later, early on a Sunday, she experienced some bleeding and was rushed to Trillium hospital. She feared the baby was lost. This could only be confirmed through an ultrasound which, as it was a long weekend, could only be carried out on the following Tuesday when staff returned, leaving a couple of agonizing days for Lisa and the rest of us.

As it happened, Ena and I were scheduled to travel to Quebec City and the Eastern Townships on the Monday for a few days, along with my sister and her husband, who were visiting us from the United Kingdom. Because of Lisa's situation, Ena didn't want to go. I managed to rearrange our itinerary slightly, postponing our departure, but only for a day. Ena was still reluctant to travel, but we persuaded her that nothing could be achieved by her remaining. And so, with heavy hearts but with valiant attempts to put a good face on it, the four of us drove to Quebec City, arriving at our hotel in the old part of the city mid-afternoon. Around four o'clock, I accessed my cell-phone messages. The reception was poor. One message was hard to interpret, but I knew it was from Lisa. Ena hurriedly called her back.

"The baby's okay," were Lisa's first words.

From then on we never took the pregnancy for granted. We faithfully kept track of the days and weeks as they passed by. As Lisa expressed it, "Dad, you couldn't remember which grade I was in at school, and yet you know precisely the number of weeks of my pregnancy! Why is that?"

Liam was born amid much celebration by the extended family, but soon after birth he contracted a respiratory virus, apparently fairly common in older babies but not for newborns. The onset was swift. Liam was quickly returned to hospital and put into isolation, but his condition deteriorated rapidly. Just hours after Liam had been admitted, Mark called us from his car. "I was on my way home from the hospital, but they've called me back. Liam stopped breathing at one point, but they managed to get him going again." We were devastated by the news. Wouldn't it be cruel to lose Liam after all that had happened? Ena called everybody she knew at home and abroad and asked them to pray for Liam.

Liam didn't improve. Lisa was in isolation with him, accompanied through the day by Ena who, because of the SARS (Severe Acute Respiratory Syndrome) outbreak in Toronto, obtained special dispensation to help look after Lisa, who had experienced a difficult birth and was not well herself. Each morning I hoped to hear of good news after the daily round by doctors, but day after day there was no progress. The doctors considered moving him to Sick Kids Hospital in Toronto to test for other, more serious causes. After about six days, Ena and Lisa thought Liam was a little better, but this hope was quickly dashed by the doctor next morning who couldn't see any improvement. Then Ena reported that the nurse thought he showed some improvement, but that, too, was not confirmed by the doctors. I became increasingly frustrated by the creation of false hopes that were then dashed by reality. Finally, after 11 long days, even the doctors said his chest was starting to clear, much to our relief. From then on, he recovered quickly and has become a strong little boy, bringing boundless joy to us.

So there I was in St. Christopher's, quietly reflecting on these events and giving thanks, when the entrance hymn began. As the service got underway, Father Scott walked over to bless the crib and talked of the joy and hope that the baby Jesus had brought into the world. I couldn't help thinking of Liam, and I could see from looking at Ena that she was, too. Father Scott ended his blessing, and I heard a rustle on my left. Lisa had arrived, with Liam in her arms. He was dressed in his warm winter suit, and his head was covered with a woolen hat that almost entirely hid his face, but not quite. One could still see his sparkling eyes, and he smiled as he caught sight of us, his arms beginning to flap as they did when he greeted someone he knew.

The tears welled up in my eyes, and I could see the tears streaming down my wife's face. Lisa caught sight of them, and she quickly became concerned. "What's the matter?" she said. "Are you all right?"

"Don't worry," Ena reassured her. "We are fine." And so we were—very fine, indeed.

Liam, November 2011, Aged 8

31

THE MAN IN TIM HORTONS

Have you ever sat opposite someone on a bus or a train or at a restaurant and wondered who they are or what they do? Some time ago, Ena and I were having our coffee (two small, one decaffeinated and the other regular, both with a little milk—too little is better than too much—and no sugar) at Tim Hortons.

We sat down with our coffees, and something about the man sitting at the table opposite caught my eye. He was eating his "chicken stew in a bread bowl" special with obvious enjoyment while reading the sports pages of Canada's national newspaper. I noticed another plate on the table, with only a serviette and a few crumbs. I deduced that he had eaten his doughnut, which as we all know comes with the combination plate, at $5.59 plus tax—a great deal. Now, I know there is nothing wrong with eating the doughnut first, but I found it odd. If he liked the doughnut best, why not leave it till the last and savour it?

The man appeared to be in his early sixties. His face was well-creased, with thin brown hair on his head, and he wore what seemed to be an attempt at a uniform. His clothes were mainly lime green, but his pants, shirt, windbreaker, and cap were various shades either side of that colour. From his belt hung a holster for a cell phone, but it was empty. Immediately, the man went up a couple of notches in my estimation.

Only a few days earlier, at the Shaw Festival, we had sat in front of a man who not only answered his cell phone just as the play was starting but also continued to negotiate the deal he was making. Most of my friends would agree that normally I am a peaceful man, but I was quite enraged by his thoughtless act. Although I am an opponent of capital punishment, I could concede a possible exception might be made for inappropriate cell-phone users! At the very least, we should have a public debate about it. But I digress.

I wondered what this green man did for living. He was clearly on his lunch break. He looked like a telephone or television repair man. I turned around and looked through the window of the coffee shop into what I could see of the parking lot. From where and what I could see, there were no vans with any identification at all. And there was no sign of any identifying company insignia on his clothes. He could have been a truck driver, but the parking lot wasn't big enough for an articulated vehicle.

I didn't get much further before a cell phone rang—a perfectly acceptable occurrence to me in Tim Hortons, I hasten to add. The man jumped up and went to the pocket of his jacket, which was hanging over the chair opposite. He activated the phone and answered with a name that I didn't catch. It could have been his name or that of his company. My curiosity was piqued, and I couldn't help but listen further. He was a man of few words, but by his tone I could tell he was anxious to satisfy whoever was on the other end of the line.

"When did it happen?" he said. "This morning around six thirty, not last night?" he questioned. Was he an undercover policeman? I wondered. No, I concluded, all policemen today are younger than me, not older.

"What was the weight?" Certainly not a policeman. "Six pounds eleven ounces" he said, taking out a pen and writing on a corner of the newspaper. This was the best clue so far. It must be something to do with a baby, but he didn't look or act like an obstetrician who had been surprised by an early delivery, nor like a grandfather, either, since he was taking it all so calmly and made no enquiries about the health of mother or baby.

"And the name?" he asked. "Melissa," he said, spelling it out loud, "M-E-L-I-S-S-A," and printing, not writing, the name out with his pen. Perhaps he was a newspaperman, taking an order for a birth notice. But why was the call made to a cell phone and not to the newspaper office? That didn't seem to solve a problem that was by now fascinating me, although I was trying to conduct myself very circumspectly.

"And the address?" he enquired. "Sixteen Cloverdale Crescent," he said again, recording it on the newspaper but without confirming the spelling. "Well, it's now Saturday morning, and it's Sunday tomorrow," he said, stating the obvious, "so it will have to be first thing Monday morning. I guarantee by eight o'clock."

"Thank you very much," he said finally and returned the phone to its holster. My curiosity was by this time almost getting the better of me. He was taking an order for something involving a baby. Could it be for a florist? But there had been no mention of what kind of flower, and I feel sure that he would have repeated it and written it down had there been such an order.

"What about a diaper delivery service?" asked Ena, who had been taking it all in almost as intently as I had. That was certainly the best guess so far, although I would have expected some company logo somewhere, and there would have been no real need to know the baby's name or birth weight.

The man sat down again and finished his meal, while we waited anxiously for him to reveal the next clue. He then meticulously tore off the corner of the newspaper he had written on, folded it into his wallet, put on his jacket, and walked out. We watched where he was going, to see if there would be another clue. Much to our annoyance, he didn't march to any of the vehicles parked where we could see. He went to the back and out of sight. We sat back, deflated; we weren't going to get the answer to the riddle, after all. We kept turning around to see if anything was coming from the rear. Nothing happened.

"Perhaps I should stroll around the back," I said to Ena.

But before she could answer, we heard the noise of an engine starting, and lo and behold, the cab of a van came into view with the green man at the wheel. It was our suspect! Then the rest of the side of the white van was gradually revealed. And there, written in bold letters, we saw "Canadian Stork Company. We Deliver", with a picture of a stork holding in its beak a diaper with a baby attached to it. That was the answer to the puzzle! The man was going to put a stork on the front lawn of 16 Cloverdale Crescent to celebrate the arrival of Melissa.

"I wonder if there will be any pink flamingos, as well," mused Ena.

32

The Cataract Operation

Ena and I have known the Browns for a long time. The wives worked together for a while, and the husbands were brought into the friendship when the women considered it safe to do so. Fortunately, John and I have a number of common interests, and we have become good friends. John has bad eyesight and developed cataracts, for which his specialist recommended surgery. As John also suffers from glaucoma, the procedure was tricky and only a few specialists were qualified to handle it. John decided to have the procedure done on his worst eye first, in a hospital east of Toronto.

As luck would have it, unexpected complications set in, and the specialist advised that another surgical procedure was necessary to save the eye. Scheduling difficulties required it to be carried out, this time, at a downtown Toronto hospital where the specialist had operating privileges. John couldn't drive, and neither could his wife, Sue, as she was herself recovering from a major operation, the kind of coincidence that you never plan for but invariably happens when least convenient.

Being a friend and recently retired, I offered to drive John. I picked him up early in the morning from his home near Guelph, and we wove our way through the rush-hour traffic, arriving at the hospital mid-morning. After an X-ray, John was examined by his specialist, who then escorted us to the eye surgery area, explaining as we went that he had added John to the list of patients scheduled for surgery that afternoon.

On our arrival at what was called the preparation room, the head nurse greeted us. John introduced me: "I would like you to meet my friend Chris who has come with me today." The nurse shook my hand warmly. As we followed her, I saw very elaborate-looking armchairs. They had headrests and footrests that could pivot, so one could lie back. They looked really comfortable. I had never seen visitors' chairs like this before.

"Please take a seat," the nurse said, and I started to lie on one.

"Oh no," the nurse said. "Those are for the patients; this is for you"— and she pointed to a little wooden chair sitting unobtrusively by the side of one of the armchairs. I sheepishly sat down, and we all chuckled at my mistake. Shortly afterwards, they came to give John some pre-op medication. John was sleepy and dozed off. One of the nurses came by and said to me, "I am sorry, but it will be a little while longer."

Eventually they came for John, and I patted his shoulder before they whisked him away. As he went, a nurse looked back at me.

"Don't worry, we'll take good care of him," she said. Another nurse said to me, "You'd be much more comfortable in the waiting room, where there's a coffee machine, magazines, and a telephone," and she showed me where it was. From time to time, one of the nurses would pass the waiting room, catch my eye, and say, "He hasn't come back yet. We'll let you know when he does." I would thank them and return to my book, thinking how attentive and considerate they were.

Little by little the waiting room emptied as family members were called to pick up their relatives, until I was the only one left. I didn't think anything of it, because I knew John was at the end of the queue, and emergencies are always possible to cause further delays.

Finally, a nurse approached me and said, "Mr. Brown's back now. He's still tired, but after a while you will be able to take him home." As I passed the nursing station, they smiled at me, and I couldn't help overhearing the end of a sentence. It was something like "been here all day. Isn't that nice?" It was then that it dawned on me. They all thought that I was John's partner. And I suppose I was being treated as though I were his next of kin. Perhaps because John wasn't part of the original operating list, the usual forms containing that information weren't there.

My first thought was one of indignation. *How could they think such a thing?* This passed quickly, to be replaced by amusement. It was quite a funny situation. It must be unusual for one middle-aged man to accompany another, and it was perhaps not unreasonable for them to draw that conclusion. Again, this thought quickly passed, and I started to imagine if I were gay, and John really was my partner, how I would feel.

I like to think my notions of tolerance and human rights are reasonably well developed. We have a few gay friends who we see occasionally, but this was different. This wasn't about how I would behave towards gays, or even how I thought others should behave. For the first time, I had been thought of as gay. And so, for a few minutes, I tried to put myself in the shoes of a gay man. The treatment John and I had received had been exemplary, but suppose that it hadn't? What if I had been automatically excluded from the preparation room? How would I have felt then? And what if the ailment had been much more severe? I tried to imagine the sadness and anger that could easily occur.

"You can take Mr. Brown home now," the nurse said, interrupting my reflection, and I helped John into the waiting wheelchair. John and I said our goodbyes, and we told each other as we left how pleasant everybody had been. Most significantly I thought, I did not choose to correct the staff on my mistaken "identity." If it didn't appear to matter to them, why should it matter to me?

It may have been John who had gone for eye surgery, but it was I who was seeing a little clearer as a result—thanks to St. Michael's Hospital.

John and me, enjoying a drink on the Zambezi River,
a mile or two upstream from Victoria Falls. Good job
we weren't in charge of navigating the boat!

33

THE ONE OF A KIND SHOW

"Would you like to come with us to the One of a Kind show?" Ena asked early one cold Saturday morning in late November. I was a bit surprised at the invitation, since I am not known for my enthusiasm towards shopping expeditions generally, and I knew that for Ena and Lisa this outing was nothing less than a mandatory annual shopping pilgrimage. But I didn't decline the invitation. I looked at the weather forecast in the paper, and I looked out of the window. I concluded that I wouldn't be able to rake any of the last remaining few leaves in the garden (leaves that were not actually mine but my neighbour's from two doors away, who hadn't bothered to rake his). I looked at the sports section and saw that the Manchester United game wasn't to be televised until Sunday. I reflected on the state of the stock market and decided I didn't want to look at the latest valuations of my portfolio. I gave them my decision.

"Yes, I will come. It's going to rain." They looked pleased, though not much flattered by my acceptance speech. They decided to take coffee and sandwiches because on previous trips they had found lining up for refreshments expensive and, perhaps more importantly, time-consuming. I bowed to their experience.

After motoring along the QEW and meandering our way through the Exhibition grounds, we entered the car park. From the advertised cost of parking, I assumed that I was about to buy a parking space in perpetuity, but no, the parking attendant cheerfully assured me, it was only for the day.

Inside the main entrance hall there was a long lineup of people waiting for the craft show to open. I led Ena and Lisa to the end of this line, but I was told that we had to buy our tickets first. I turned around and saw there was another long line to buy the tickets. I muttered something under my breath about this being very inefficient and bureaucratic, and I was told by my companions in no uncertain terms that, although a guest of theirs, I was not free to spoil their day with such petty comments. I was well and truly put in my place.

We paid, and at last we entered the showroom proper. Immediately I was conscious of Dean Martin singing "Christmas Bells." We picked up a ballot for a draw for something or other, and I was about to make a comment that we were simply providing our names for another marketing mailing list. In light of my earlier warning, I thought better of it. I didn't want to be sent home so early.

I estimated from the program that there were 750 "artists, artisans, and designers" to visit, and I calculated that it represented for me one year's shopping quota, all in one day. The aisles were marked from A to Y. Thinking that it will be the least crowded, we decided to start at Y and work our way back to A. We found that Y was where most of the food stalls were congregated, and there were lots of free handouts. I didn't know that chocolate could cover so many things, from nuts to berries! And so we began.

Already the show was busy. We decided on a strategy should we get parted. We would meet beside the large real Christmas tree in the middle of the showroom. And then, as if we had been overheard, there was a public address announcement that proceeded to give everybody else the same advice! A darker consequence of what can befall those lost was described by a sign at one booth that read "Abandoned children will be sold as slaves."

Although I was expecting it, I couldn't help but notice the preponderance of women in every combination you could imagine. There were teenage girls in clusters with their friends, mothers with daughters, grandmothers with their daughters and granddaughters, and groups of elderly women. There were a few families, some trailing reluctant little boys and fathers. There were a few young men, but those usually had their arms wrapped around their girlfriends and were generally oblivious to their surroundings. I decided to carry out a little survey of my own. I stood at one spot for a minute and counted those passing by. I determined that men were outnumbered ten to one. As if to make the point, I even heard one man comment to another on the high level of estrogen. I thought to myself: *He's brave, and perhaps a little foolish, to have said it out loud.*

I learned very quickly that my role was to carry the purchases, and I was soon laden. At one point I was able to sit down for a few moments. At the other end of the bench was slumped a heavy middle-aged man, half-asleep. A teenage girl with a blonde ponytail, dressed in the latest hip jeans that showed the requisite midriff below her top, approached the man. She came over and shook him.

"Wake up, Daddy," she said. "It's time to move on." He got up somewhat reluctantly, though he tried to put a good face on it, and shuffled off with his daughter while she animatedly described her latest purchases. Ena and Lisa joined me on the bench, and we ate our lunch. Even though we were indoors, it felt like a picnic, and passersby looked enviously at our simple cheese sandwiches.

There seemed to be an infinite variety in the goods being sold: candles, stained glass, children's toys, jewellery, pottery, and embroidery. I was amazed at how even scraps of wood could be used to create lamps or sculptures. Some looked quite artistic, while others, like the clocks with faces made out of wax, looked odd. I walked on ahead. At one corner, I saw a stall laden with what I thought was incredibly gaudy and ugly jewellery, but it was surrounded by women. The man behind the stall was wearing a wide necklace to advertise his wares, and he was obviously enjoying the non-stop banter with his customers.

I heard a woman saying in frustration to another, "I've been here since 10:00, and I haven't bought anything yet!" Some people brought high-tech aids with them. One woman was speaking loudly into her cell phone, "I'm in row K now. I'll meet you at the north end of row P in five minutes."

Eventually, by about 3:00 in the afternoon, Ena and Lisa decided that they could not walk another step. Luckily for me, this happened to coincide with the fact that there were no more booths to visit. We were ready to go. My job was to retrieve the car. To the sound of Jose Feliciano wishing me "Feliz Navidad" in English and Spanish, I walked out of the showroom clutching some of the purchases. I carried three wrought-iron angels (a large one for the garden and two for the house); a lamp with a parchment shade, a gift for my daughter, which we had been pretending to hide from her all day; some ceramic wine goblets; and a variety of pottery bowls. In response to my enquiry, I was assured that all were essential for our continued existence on this earth, and without them our lives would be irreparably worse!

My womenfolk clambered into the car when I picked them up, flushed with success. As I drove away, Ena turned to Lisa and said, "I can't wait till next year." They didn't ask me for my views.

I think it's very likely that I'll have something else to do on that day! I told myself.

34

AN INVITATION TO DINNER

"Hi, Dad—what's up?" I heard Martin say breezily when I picked up the telephone one Sunday evening.

"Fine," I said in response to his implied question.

"Would you and Mum like to come over for dinner with Janice and me on Friday?"

"Let me check with my social director," which I did, as she was sitting right by the telephone. As I relayed the message, her eyebrows rose, and I could tell she was thinking the same thing I was.

Martin and Janice had known each other for more than a year, and their relationship seemed to be going well. There were promising signs. First, Martin seemed very relaxed and confident when he brought her over to meet us for family dinners and suchlike, and then they went to Cuba on vacation together. We liked Janice immensely and thought they were a good couple. We had been at Martin's house before but generally for something more informal. This invitation was different.

"Do you think they are going to announce their engagement?" asked Ena, cutting to the chase straightaway, with no beating about the bush.

"It certainly does seem possible," I admitted, cautiously trying to dampen expectations but believing she was probably right.

"It would be so nice to see Martin settled with someone he loves."

"I agree, but let's not get too ahead of ourselves. Next thing you will want me to take a bottle of champagne with us so we can celebrate," I said jokingly.

"That's a really good idea," said Ena enthusiastically, "but I wouldn't want to embarrass them by taking it in with us when we arrive. Let's leave it in the car and bring it in when they make the announcement." We left our speculation at that, but as I looked over at her, I could tell her mind was working in overdrive. A few minutes later, the telephone rang. We looked at each other but didn't say a word. I picked up the telephone. It was Lisa.

"Guess what?" Lisa said excitedly. It could be anything: one of the boys was sick, Mark's back was acting up, someone at school had done something really bad or really good in her history class, or the house next door had sold for well over the asking price. I tried all those answers and others, but none was right.

"I give up," I conceded.

"Martin's invited us over for dinner on Friday with you guys."

Has he indeed? I said to myself, overlooking the irreverent reference to her parents. That certainly was significant. I quickly realized my skills would be totally inadequate to do justice to the subsequent discussion with Lisa, an expert in nuances associated with family matters and the analysis of the implications associated with this dinner invitation. I therefore passed the receiver immediately over to Ena, who had gleaned from my expression the purpose of the call.

The conclusions of their long conversation, as summarized by Ena afterwards, were as follows: first, that it was an announcement of their engagement; second, that we should (obviously) act surprised, following with fervent and genuine expressions of congratulations; third, that champagne in the car was a good idea as long as I ensured that on the one hand it was chilled and on the other it wasn't so chilled as to freeze; finally, that Lisa and Mark would be overdoing it to bring flowers, and furthermore, just in case we were wrong, champagne could keep for another occasion, whereas flowers might be wasted. Spontaneity was critical.

Through the week Lisa and my wife checked in several times to see if there were further developments requiring a change to the game plan. There weren't. I like plans to be robust, and this plan seemed perfect. Excitement mounted through the week. As we prepared to go out on Friday, the inevitable problem came up.

"It's difficult to know what to wear," said Ena as though this were some new phenomenon and not daily routine.

"Why?" I was foolish enough to ask, because I usually regard it as a rhetorical question.

"Well, it's a special occasion, and yet I don't want to go too dressed up. It will mean that we have been anticipating it, and I want it to be a surprise."

Ena eventually selected something to wear, and we left. We were both excited, but I was trying to conceal it more than Ena was. Martin and Janice greeted us warmly at the door and, as if it had been synchronized, which of course it had, along came Lisa and Mark in their car. Janice and Martin looked well and happy, and we exchanged surreptitious glances between the rest of us when neither of them was looking. One detail on which we were unsure was the timing of the announcement. Was it going to be at the beginning? I leaned toward the beginning, after which everyone could relax; to the ladies' thinking, nearer the end would be a climax to the evening.

We had some lovely appetizers and a drink before we sat down to dinner. No announcement yet. Martin poured the wine for dinner, and I thought, *This is it.* But it wasn't, and we continued with the meal. Only after dessert, when the coffee had been poured, did Martin call the party to order.

"I suppose you have been wondering," he began, "why we have invited you here this evening." We feigned surprise that they would think that. "We are so glad you were able to come," he continued, "because Janice and I have an announcement to make." We all started smiling, anticipating the punch line. "We were wondering," he said, looking at Ena and me, "how you would like," and he paused again—we thought so he could remember what came next, something along the lines of "Janice to be your daughter-in-law." Instead of this, he said, in a firm voice, "How you would like to be grandparents again." That was it! They were expecting a baby! Well, of course that wasn't what we had been expecting, and I suppose our faces might have gone vacant for the briefest of moments before we burst into congratulations and some of us wiped emerging tears from our eyes. The promise of a new baby is a wonderful event, and we were very happy for them and for us. Needless to say, the champagne came out to celebrate.

We had no doubt that they would get married in due course and in their own time, which happened a few months later. A few more months later Damon arrived on the scene, and three years later along came Tyler, to make four beautiful and precious grandsons with which Ena and I are blessed.

Curiously, Janice and Martin have never asked us how we managed to have champagne in our car that evening.

Janice, Martin, and Damon—the surprise
guest at the dinner party!

35

ROTARY AND THE

KHETHOKUHLE CHILD CARE CENTRE

We had been in the air-conditioned minivan for two hours, as it wove its way west of Durban in South Africa, first across motorways, then across lesser roads, and finally on dusty, dirt-track roads over the rolling countryside of KwaZulu-Natal province, in South Africa. We had known it would be hot and humid, because it had been like that when we set off from our comfortable hotel on the shores of the Indian Ocean—where at least there was a breeze—and we had expected it to get even hotter. Along the road we passed many smallholdings, a hut with an enclosure for an animal or two, a few old cars, and occasionally a fragile-looking line of electricity poles. We noticed the poles particularly, because they were so unusual here, whereas in Canada there are so many overhead wires and cables that, after a while, we block them out.

Just as many of the women in our party were beginning to wonder where they could possibly go to the bathroom, we started to weave our way down into a valley, where those of us sitting on the left side could see a gathering of people, a tent, and a banner very familiar to us, that of Rotary. As we drew closer, we saw smiling faces, mostly women and children wearing gaily coloured dresses and uniforms, but only a few men. Our van pulled up alongside a few other similar vehicles. We had arrived. We clutched our water bottles, Tilley hats, sunglasses, and cameras, in that order, checked that we had smothered ourselves in sunscreen, and prepared to emerge into the heat. David Martindale, our bearded Rotarian guide from Kitchener, who had been instrumental in organizing what we were about to witness, said, "Welcome to Khethokuhle!" as he opened the doors and we disembarked.

All this was a far cry from my Rotary club in Mississauga. My links to Rotary go back to the 1940s, when my father became a member in Northwich, England. He became president of his club in 1956 and later was made an honorary member when he became ill. From the time I grew up I could remember the Rotary motto: Service Above Self, which made a great impression on me at the time. My mother was also very supportive of Rotary and was active in the Inner Wheel, serving as president of her club, as indeed has my sister, Christine. I always thought I would become a Rotarian one day. The opportunity presented itself when my brother-in-law, Michael, became a Rotarian and, in the summer of 1995 when he visited what is now my club, he met Gord Patterson, one of my neighbours, who invited me to join.

I enjoy going to Rotary on Tuesday evenings. Where else can you get a warm welcome among friends, share a meal, conduct some Rotary business that usually benefits someone somewhere in the world, perhaps listen to a stimulating speaker, have some fun or perhaps even a debate, all within the space of a couple of hours? But there is more to Rotary than attending meetings.

People join Rotary for different reasons. I joined primarily because of community service. I enjoy working with other Rotarians on work parties. It could be helping clean up a local park on a frosty day when the snow is swirling around. It could be painting at an apartment in a local women's shelter, making it look a little more inviting to a woman and her children desperate for safe shelter. It could be taking a Christmas hamper to a needy family. Apart from the satisfaction derived from helping others, you get to know your Rotary colleagues better.

I have been very proud to present on behalf of our club significant cheques to local hospitals; these have resulted from our efforts at car raffles and wine-tasting events. Selling tickets can be tedious, but being paired with another Rotarian can make it tolerable and even pleasant. And you meet interesting people. I remember once when a middle-aged man, quite emaciated, came to buy a ticket for a car raffle to benefit the oncology department of a local hospital. The man told us he was dying of lung cancer and had only weeks to live, but he said he wanted to buy a ticket, even though the date of the draw was way beyond his life expectancy, because, he said, "Rotary does good work." Another time, some hairdressers from a local salon came to us one day and donated a significant amount of money because it was the end of Ramadan, and as Moslems they were expected to do something to help those less fortunate, and they "knew" Rotary would use the money wisely. All Rotarians have similar anecdotes.

I enjoy hearing from students who have benefitted from the variety of programs offered by Rotary, such as scholarship and citizenship awards and annual conference and exchange programs. Invariably these students give us hope and confidence that the future is in good hands.

Rotary is also very active internationally. Some Rotarians are heavily involved with the worldwide eradication of polio, travelling to assist with inoculations, or with volunteering directly in numerous projects to alleviate poverty, illiteracy, hunger, and thirst around the globe.

In 2007, Ena and I had the opportunity to visit South Africa with other Rotarians. Part of the trip was vacation and part was to visit some projects that Rotary had been supporting, to meet those involved and to see firsthand how the projects were doing. The vacation part was a great success. South Africa is a stunningly beautiful country. But what made the trip particularly memorable for us was a visit to a community child care centre near Molweni, just west of Durban, where the HIV/AIDS pandemic is particularly acute and where grandmothers and other relatives are caring for orphans. These centres provide basic nutrition, education, and child care in sanitary and safe facilities. The program was founded by South Africa Rotarians in partnership with the non-profit Soul of Africa, and it has been a remarkable success story.

Our visit was arranged to coincide with the opening of the Khethokuhle ("to look after well") child care centre. The Soul of Africa funded the bricks and mortar to build the child care centre, while Rotary paid for toilets, water tanks, kitchen equipment, furniture, educational material, and teaching aids. Rotary also monitors expenditures and provides hands-on volunteer help.

On our arrival, we could see immediately what we had travelled to celebrate: a modest single-storey building that is palatial compared to the rusting tin shack 50 yards away that had been used before. This was a day of celebration, with local dignitaries attending, and a large tent had been erected for the opening ceremony. For us, it was special because of the children and the grandmothers. The centre cares for children from 3 months up to 5 years old. The older children were beautifully dressed in crisp uniforms and were all smiles, though some were understandably a little shy when we approached them. Some gathered around, giggling, to see pictures of them taken by Rotarians with digital cameras. We saw grandmothers demonstrating the making of sandals, which are sold through Soul of Africa, thereby providing a source of income for them. Many Rotarians brought sandals home.

Nearly all of the grandmothers had lost children to the HIV/AIDS pandemic, but one grandmother symbolized for all of us their plight. For some reason, I have associated the woman in the photograph, taken by Ena, with the name of Grace, although it is highly unlikely that could have been her name. We learned that Grace had lost four children to HIV/ AIDS and now was bringing up 12 grandchildren. The picture shows the face of a woman who has borne a lot of sorrow; she is aged beyond her years, yet she still displays the quiet dignity and firm determination to work for a better life for her grandchildren. We all know how precious grandchildren are, and Grace and others like her deserve all the help we can give them.

It was impossible not to shed a few tears that day. Ena and I were impressed and humbled by the generosity of local Rotarians involved in this project, and gratified that our own club was also a supporter. Never have I felt that my dollars were better spent than on that day, and I increasingly feel the need for Rotarians to place a higher emphasis on international service. I have heard some say that the problems of the world are so large and complex that only governments and large corporations can deal with them. We are learning, however, through recent experience, that their capabilities are limited, and perhaps some problems are so big that they are best handled community by community, with local help. This is where Rotary comes in.

Joining Rotary is one of the best decisions I have ever made. I am proud to be a Rotarian.

"Grace"

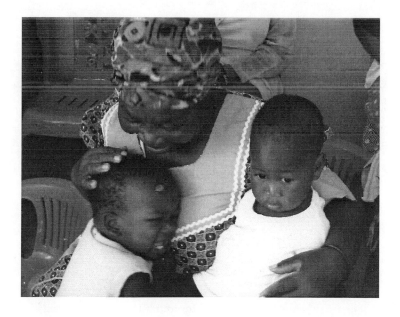

Two children and their grandmother

The "old" child care centre. Photograph by David Martindale

The "new" child care centre. Photograph by David Martindale

36

GOD BLESS TOM

I have always been fascinated by the Second World War. Nothing can stimulate my interest as much as the latest revelation about the state of mind of Hitler, or the conspiracy theory surrounding Pearl Harbor, or just the incredible logistical complexity of D-day. My growing up in England in the forties and fifties may have something to do with it, although I was too young to have any personal reminiscences of the war. After it was over, I remember seeing convoys of tanks passing our house, and we always gave a lift to anyone wearing a uniform. My family was not seriously affected by the war, unlike others who suffered grievously. My father was an electrical engineer in a reserved occupation deemed essential to the war effort. We lived in a peaceful village in Cheshire, which remained peaceful except for the occasional stray bomb and the activity caused by its proximity to Patton's headquarters. In contrast, Manchester, only fifteen miles away, where my cousins, Shirley and Gordon, lived, was subjected to many bombing raids; one could still see the damage they caused many years later.

We had a large garden where Dad grew vegetables and kept a few hens, and my mother bottled the various fruits that were picked from our trees. Dad was in the home guard, and my siblings and I were later to play with his wooden rifle, as well as the family gas masks that, fortunately, had not been needed and what remained of the ration books that, unfortunately, had been. My parents talked about the war with nostalgia for what I can only describe now as a single-minded unity of purpose, which gripped and unified the population at the time, and which they found—notwithstanding all the worry and uncertainty—compelling and stimulating. As I grew up, I read many books about the war. Later, I subscribed to a weekly magazine detailing the political, military, and social aspects of the Second World War. When I immigrated to Canada in 1969, all 156 magazines, neatly bound in eight black binders with gold embossed lettering, occupied an important place in my trunk, and they still grace a bookshelf in my office.

Remembrance Day is important and relevant to me. But where have I been at the 11th hour on the 11th day of the 11th month? Mostly I have either been watching the television coverage at home, because as a member of a government agency for a time I had the undeserved good fortune to have the day off, or I have just stood alone in my office at 11:00, wearing my poppy. But I have never actually been to a Remembrance Day ceremony at a cenotaph, until this year, when I decided, now that I am retired, that I would attend one.

When Remembrance Day arrived, I had second thoughts and toyed with the idea of watching the national ceremony in Ottawa on television, as usual. About ten thirty, I changed my mind. I pulled on my coat, hat, and scarf and hurried down to Port Credit. I was lucky to find a parking spot behind the hockey arena, and I walked up to the cenotaph. I picked what I thought would be a good vantage point and watched the last-minute preparations: one veteran, presumably the official musician, was getting his keyboard ready; a minister was testing the microphone; flag bearers were gathering together, grinning at each other, no doubt reminiscing as they did so; and the police officers were doing their best to get lined up for the parade. Some veterans, many obviously frail, were already seated in chairs, accompanied by caring wives or adult children who fussed over them, adjusting their scarves and seeking reassurances they were comfortable.

And then the ceremony began. Four air force cadets, with gleaming boots and pressed uniforms, marched slowly, under the measured instructions of their equally youthful officer, to their positions at the four corners of the cenotaph. Before long, the hustle and bustle of everyday life was broken by the minute's silence, and the crowd, now several hundred strong, bowed their heads in the autumn sunshine among falling leaves that swirled around in the occasional gusts.

It was a very peaceful, moving moment, and I reflected that across many countries, in countless cities, towns, and villages, ceremonies just like this one were being held to remember the fallen. My eyes watered over, and I was glad when the various dignitaries and service organizations began laying the wreaths. The federal MP was first, followed by the MPP, and then various service organizations and service clubs. This went on for some time. Conversations started to break out, and I saw people shuffling their feet, perhaps getting cold or perhaps getting impatient for the service to end.

And then Tom Jackson was introduced. I forget who or what he was representing, but I remember his name. He was wheeled forward in a chair by two men. He had two shawls around him, a red one and a grey one. He wore a beret, and he was hunched forward in the chair, as though his chest was weighted down by the dazzling array of medals displayed upon it. A wreath rested on his knees. He was pushed to the steps of the cenotaph. His two attendants tried to take the wreath from him, with the obvious intention of saving him the trouble of laying the wreath himself. Tom would have none of it. He remonstrated with them and then gripped the sides of the wheelchair and lifted himself up. He was virtually carried up the steps, where he placed the wreath along with the others. All chattering had stopped and every eye was now on Tom.

Even with assistance, Tom had great difficulty navigating the steps back to his chair, where his attendants attempted to seat him. He again protested and then, mustering perhaps all the strength he had left in his body, he stood upright, faced the cenotaph, and brought his right hand, slowly and shaking, to his forehead, giving a salute to his fallen comrades. By now tears were streaming down my face, and those around me were similarly moved. As Tom finished his salute and fell back into his chair, one man to my left at the back began to clap. His neighbour joined in, followed by a young couple from the other side of the cenotaph. Within seconds the gesture spread, until everyone was clapping, and the applause did not stop until Tom had returned to his starting place. At that moment, for all of us, this determined old veteran had become the symbol of what we were there to celebrate.

I shall never forget that Remembrance Day.

Five days after I wrote this, on November 28, Tom died, at the age of 85. I know now he was a paratrooper with the First Canadian Battalion, who jumped into the Normandy darkness on D-Day, June 6, 1944, and later into the Battle of the Rhine.

God bless you, Tom. And thanks.

Tom Jackson, assisted by his two sons, November 11, 2008.
Photograph provided by RJ Entertainment Publishing

An edited version of this story was published in *The Mississauga News* on December 10, 2008.

37

SELLING THE FRIDGE

"Should we put an ad in the paper?" I asked.

"Let's advertise them on *craigslist*, "Ena suggested. "That's how everyone sells these days," she added, as if to clinch the matter.

"Do you know how?" said I, ever the Luddite, wondering if the time spent would be worth the effort but knowing that the bait would be hard to resist.

"I can easily find out," was the retort.

What were we selling? A fridge, a white stove with ceramic top, a matching hood with extract fan and microwave, a white dishwasher, a solid oak table with six accompanying chairs—all, as the ad said, in perfect working condition.

Why were we selling them? We were gutting the kitchen, and everything in it was going: furniture, appliances, lighting, cupboards—the lot. Our task was to get rid of them, and the prices we quoted were reasonable in the first place and completely negotiable in the second place.

Most of the kitchen was more than 30 years old, with a refit some 14 years ago to paint the cupboards, put on a new countertop, and some other refinements, which had worked well but had only delayed the inevitable. The kitchen is a critical room in our house because we both like to cook and we entertain a lot, even if most of it is for family. We sometimes refer to the kitchen as the "food factory," although that reflects more of the volume prepared than quality. We had saved up for a new kitchen, well, for some of it, anyway. Ena had put aside money she had earned when asked to fill in for a maternity leave at the place she had worked before retiring.

The design work had been long and occasionally frustrating, but in the end satisfying, and we were pleased with the progress. The renovation was proceeding quickly. All the sale items were cluttering up the garage, and as long as they remained, they reminded us of the old kitchen. We wanted to turn a new page, not to mention end the inconvenience of not being able to park a car! Disposing of the stove was easy. It turned out Lisa wanted it, and we arranged for two men to pick it up and deliver it to her house, agreeing to take her stove in return, which helped.

Soon—surprisingly so, though I could not admit it—the ad was up and running on *craigslist*, and the e-mails came thick and fast from across the GTA.

"Interested in the dishwasher but can only pay $75. Is there room to negotiate?" Jim, from Milton. There was room, but not if that was his limit. There were others.

"How big is the table?" Ashok, Oakville.

"Will be along to pick up the fridge tomorrow night." Fred, Brampton.

"Very interested in the fridge. Is it still available?" Deidre, Mississauga.

"How old is the dishwasher? Can you give me the specifications?" Ranji, Orangeville.

It looked very promising, and Ena was kept busy responding, measuring, looking up manuals, and giving out our phone number to those she considered promising prospects. We thought we would at least dispose of the fridge quickly. The next evening we stayed in to await the arrival of Fred from Brampton, and while we were waiting we rehearsed negotiating strategies and pricing options. We needn't have bothered. Alas, Fred from Brampton didn't show up. We soon found out why.

"Sorry I couldn't come last night. I had a flat tire, and my spare was flat, as well. The CAA took ages to get to me, and my wife couldn't pick me up, because she was at her sister's, who has just had a baby." The e-mail went on and on before coming to the point: "Is the fridge still available? If it is, I'll come at the weekend." Fred, Brampton. Plausible reason, if more than we needed to know, we thought. We'd give him the benefit of the doubt. As we expected, there were no enquiries about the hood and microwave. We had two enquiries about the table, but the size had probably put them off.

The following evening we had pleasant surprise. Ranji from Orangeville turned up with a van. He was a qualified electrician, gave the dishwasher a quick inspection, and offered us close to the asking price. Within a few minutes the deal was closed to everyone's satisfaction, and the dishwasher disappeared to Orangeville. We were pleased and hoped it would be the prelude to the rest going. But it wasn't. We received one or two more e-mails from Fred of Brampton continuing his life story, but it seemed he had lost interest or the means of transportation.

Just as we were beginning to give up hope, another e-mail came in one Tuesday, enquiring about the fridge. "If in good condition, would be prepared to make an offer around $180. Let me know if it is still available." Richard, Scarborough.

"Still available," Ena advised, resisting the temptation to say there was a lot of interest.

"Will come on Saturday afternoon, if convenient."

"Okay, but trust you will understand if we get an acceptable offer in the meantime, in which case I will advise you," Ena said.

Saturday came, and about two o'clock a late-model Toyota SUV rolled up the driveway, towing a trailer. A good-looking couple in their early thirties climbed out and introduced themselves. This was Richard from Scarborough and his wife. After we had introduced ourselves, Richard said, "I forgot to unfasten our daughter" and went back to his car, opened the back door, and brought out their daughter. She was two years old, a pretty little dark-haired girl wearing an equally pretty blue-checked dress. She smiled, and as often happens when children are around, the atmosphere became more relaxed. They seemed a nice modern family.

I opened the garage and showed them the fridge, which Richard inspected while we explained the various features. He asked why we were selling it, and we explained, pointing to the other items as corroboration.

"Does it work?" he asked.

"Yes, I can plug it in if you would like me to show you," I offered.

'That won't be necessary." He consulted briefly with his wife, who had been chatting with Ena about bringing up children and family life, while their daughter was playing with a ball she had discovered in the garage.

"The fridge looks in good condition, and I'll offer $170." It wasn't a bad offer, and we were able to quickly settle for $180. He promptly pulled out his wallet and counted the notes. We were pleased, and they seemed pleased as well, as much with the atmosphere surrounding the transaction as the deal itself.

"While you're here, is there anything else that might interest you?" asked Ena. They weren't interested in the microwave or the table. They looked at the old kitchen light fixture. It was in good shape, but we weren't sure what we were going to do with it and had excluded it from the sale. It wasn't worth much, so we said they could have it. It meant one thing less for us to worry about, and it felt like a sale though no money had changed hands.

We helped Richard load the fridge onto his trailer and he tied it on. We wished them well as we said goodbye, and they drove off, Ena and I reflecting on what an enjoyable half-hour we had spent with them. Selling could make you feel good, we said to ourselves. We were not prepared for the e-mail we received a day later.

"The fridge doesn't work. I am getting a friend of mine to look at it," came from Richard of Scarborough. We were stunned. The fridge had been working well when we'd put it in the garage. We wondered if he was setting us up, although that didn't reconcile with our image of the person we had met.

Later that day came another e-mail. This gave a report from his friend, with pictures that were hard to understand, but evidently the freezing material had leaked out and couldn't easily be replaced. The e-mail concluded, "I bought the fridge on the understanding that it worked, so I would like my money back." Ena and I considered our position. Usually it is "buyer beware" in these transactions, and it was possible the fridge had been damaged in transporting it to Scarborough or putting it in its new location. Furthermore, we had said that the fridge was working and had offered to plug it in for him, which he declined. However, we didn't want to create a situation in which the fridge got dumped back on our driveway. We debated whether to take a hard line and reply that it was his tough luck, or whether we should give him his money back.

That evening, at my Rotary club meeting, there was a delay in setting up the computer equipment for the speaker, so I took the opportunity of briefly summarizing the problem to my fellow Rotarians and asked them for advice, because the practice of sound ethics is an important part of being a Rotarian. I received a mix of advice, but no consensus. Of course, none of them were actually facing the situation or had met the couple in question. I reported back to Ena. Again we reviewed the situation. It was also possible that the fridge had been damaged in moving it from the kitchen to the garage or while it was unplugged in our garage for several weeks. We couldn't be sure. We decided that he was telling the truth about the fridge not working, whatever the cause. This was the only thing that made sense, and it reconciled with our personal recollection of him, little though that admittedly was. After much reflection, we made a decision. Ena replied to Richard of Scarborough.

"We believed that the fridge was working when we sold it, and we offered to demonstrate that to you. However, we accept your assurance that the fridge is not working now. As a result, we are prepared to return half your money. This is our final offer." We received an immediate reply.

"I accept that you sold it in good faith and that it was part of my responsibility to have fully checked that the fridge was working properly. I appreciate your offer and accept it," said Richard of Scarborough. We wrote out a cheque for $90 and sent it off. We were comfortable with our decision. Case closed. What would you have done?

What about the microwave and the table? Our enthusiasm for selling had waned. We donated the microwave to Habitat for Humanity, and the table is gracing our basement as a games table for our grandsons.

38

Coping with my Stutter

I have stuttered all my life. There are only a few minutes in my day when I don't think about what I am going to say next or how to say it.

My earliest recollections are of mimicry at school in the playground. Not that it was done with any malicious intent. It's just the way children are, but it hurt nevertheless. I was lucky to have close friends in school who learned not to finish my sentences—which is tempting and can be awkward if the listener guesses wrong.

Although my teachers were all supportive, I experienced moments of sheer panic. I had difficulty with consonants: *w* (what), *c* (cat), *t* (two), *d* (do), particularly if they were in the first words I spoke. The teachers called us by our surnames, and at the beginning of a term a new teacher, in an effort to learn our names, would go up and down the rows asking each boy to say his name. As they approached me, I rehearsed in my mind how I would say mine. Invariably, when my turn came at last, I was in such a state that I often stumbled over the *Ch* in my name. Eventually I would get it out, but I would be drenched in sweat, as the inevitable wave of embarrassment washed over me. I fancifully thought of changing my name to make it easier for me to pronounce!

Similarly, when we had to give our marks on tests to a teacher so he could record them, I was fine if it was an easy number like 8 or 16, but 10 or 21 could be difficult. I often thought of changing the mark, even to a lower number, just to avoid the situation. But I never did.

I never put my hand up in class to answer questions. Once when a teacher asked me something, I remember stuttering over the letter *w*, in well, to start my answer. After I had finally got it out, the teacher said, "That was a lot of effort for just 'well.'" He was right, of course.

Outside school, tasks trivial to others were major ordeals for me: asking for a train ticket, running errands to the local shop for my mother, or buying candies. Worst of all was using the telephone; it still is to some extent, and this is common to most stutterers. I will do almost anything to avoid using the telephone.

When I was eight, my mother took me to speech therapy classes in a nearby town. I didn't like going there and found other things that helped, instead. Stutterers never stutter when singing, but I have a lousy voice, and life is not a musical. Reading poetry, however, was useful, because the rhythm seemed to lubricate my speech. So I read a lot of poetry, and by the age of nine I could recite quite comfortably at Sunday school concerts, much to the amazement of people who knew me. Although the moments prior to such appearances were nerve-racking, these performances gave me confidence, and I looked for similar opportunities to develop my speech.

I could read text quite well and was lucky enough to win several reading prizes at school. I discovered that extensive preparation paid off. Sometimes if I saw a problem word in a text, I would substitute another word that was easier for me. Stutterers are inventive and often have a large vocabulary because they are always looking for synonyms.

Until I was about fifteen, I was particularly shy, but it is the stutter that makes one shy, not vice versa. As I got into my twenties and began work, my fluency improved but still had its moments sometimes when I least expected it. Asking for things like "two coffees" is difficult. My relief at getting it out right, perhaps with some filler words at the beginning, such as "Please can I have two coffees?" can be dashed when the listener says, "Sorry, I didn't get that. Can you repeat it?" When all eyes are on you, repetitions are excruciating.

In everyday conversation with friends or family, I am fluent most of the time, but cocktail parties with new people sometimes drive my anxiety level up.

Over time, I became an effective public speaker. Paradoxically, my stutter has helped in a couple of ways. Little did an audience know that for me to deliver a good presentation at work it took hours of preparation and practice. This helped me know my stuff, which enhanced my credibility and gave me confidence when I appeared before regulatory bodies to explain company positions.

I've also found e-mail a boon as an option to the telephone. I never fell into the trap of using it exclusively, though. Instead, I've made a point of going to another person's office to discuss a complex problem or delicate issue face to face. As a result, my management style became more effective, and I developed a reputation for having strong interpersonal skills.

Now that I am in my sixties, my stutter doesn't bother me as much. I am just more sanguine about it, partly because I can reflect on a wonderful family and interesting career, and partly because I can avoid or control most of the situations where it can trip me up. For example, I never use the intercom to give my order at a drive-through coffee shop. Instead, I park my car and go inside, where I can deal person to person. I suppose my stutter and I have reached a kind of truce—it's there, but it doesn't much get in the way of my life.

When King George VI died in 1952, Winston Churchill sent a floral tribute with the simple inscription "For Valour." Most thought that it referred to his leadership of his country through the Second World War. I think it was for coping with his severe stutter. Nothing, not even Hitler, could terrify him as much as the risk of stuttering in public. He deserved an Oscar, only he wasn't acting.

Illustration by Dushan Milic

This story was published, along with the illustration, in *The Globe and Mail*, on March 1, 2011, a day after Colin Firth won the Oscar for his portrayal of King George VI in *The King's Speech*.

39

TAKING PICTURES

Ena loves taking pictures. They are usually in one of three categories: family; vacations; gardens and flowers. Let me declare my bias at the outset. I enjoy looking at pictures, for a while anyway, although I am not particularly keen on seeing Aunt Nellie or a Queen Elizabeth hybrid tea rose (these are hypothetical examples, I hasten to add, since we have neither) from ten different angles, but I become impatient with the process of taking pictures—the camera adjustments, the posing and such—that takes away any semblance of spontaneity.

At one time I used 35 mm film, but Ena got fed up with all my pictures of hills and castles ("There aren't any people," she would say) and with the difficulty in looking at the slides. Either she had to hold the slides up to the light to get some idea of what the pictures were or wait for the biennial slide show in which images were displayed on a plain wall—or a sheet, or later a collapsible screen, with the projector perched precariously on top of a pile of books, since none of our tables were the right height.

I preferred using a manual slide projector to an automatic one. The latter always seemed to jam. In either case, loading the carousel was a problem. Putting the slides back to front and upside down, or whatever it is, was an impossible task to carry out successfully for 100 or more slides, not to mention the added risk of slides slipping out of the carousel if not fastened properly. No wonder slides were for special performances only! Furthermore, and perhaps this became the final straw for Ena, you can't pass slides around to show friends what your grandchildren look like.

So Ena acquired her own camera, and the responsibility for taking pictures—and I mean actual photographs, not slides—at family events or vacations was happily transferred to her. I have almost given up my attempts completely, except where my trained eye sees the potential for a scenic photograph and I commission Ena to take it to my specifications. Sometimes when I do that Ena seems to be a bit reluctant to accept the assignment and has been known to say, "Take it yourself!" But to be fair, Ena has produced in the recent past some wonderful photographs in her subject categories. Many of them are placed carefully into albums that can be readily accessed when required, and she has used many of them to produce cards for birthdays and special occasions, or notelets to give to friends as gifts.

There is one problem with photography that is common to all. There you are, at a scenic spot, with your wife, or with your grandchildren in a particularly cute pose, and there's no one to take the picture. Fortunately, someone usually comes along, and you can ask them if they would mind taking your picture. Most of the time, they agree quite easily.

"Certainly," they say, "I'd be glad to." And they take the picture. The only trouble is that some people are better at taking pictures than others. With anyone using an unfamiliar camera there is always the risk of under- or overexposure, a head chopped off, or bodies sliced in half. In the old days, you would wait until after the vacation, when you got the pictures back from the developer and eagerly looked at the pictures, only to find out that the snap you were particularly proud of—the one where the leaning Tower of Pisa is apparently sprouting from the top of your head—hadn't come out as expected.

The advent of the digital camera has revolutionized the business of taking pictures. Now, you can see whether the picture you have just taken is any good or not, and if it isn't, you can retake it. You can take multiple shots, so you can pick the best and delete the others. You can create, in conjunction with a computer or an iPod, a fancy picture show on the television or computer screen—Ena is very good at these, with the pictures coming into view at different angles, so it doesn't get boring, and music accompanying the show. Of course, technology is constantly changing. Now you can take pictures with your mobile phone. You can easily fake pictures, as well. We have a great picture of Ena and me in evening dress. It looks very natural. In fact, it is a composite of two pictures, one of Ena and one of me, taken separately but cleverly combined by our daughter-in-law, Janice. *The camera doesn't lie?* Sure it can!

This past summer Ena (a new digital camera in hand) and I accompanied our daughter, her husband, Mark, and their two children, Liam and Luke, to the United Kingdom for three weeks. I will not go into any detail on that trip here. Suffice it to say we had a great time. Those interested in more information will find very interesting and illuminating the seven-volume account of our vacation that will undoubtedly be published in due course—with photographs!

One day, from our base in Nantwich, a pretty market town in Cheshire, we travelled to the Wirral Peninsula, skirting the City of Chester. Ena and I had decided to visit the village of Port Sunlight, while the others visited a nearby aquarium, the particular attraction being the sharks, which were second only to dinosaurs in interest to our grandsons.

Port Sunlight is a village built in the late 19ᵗʰ century by the Lever brothers, the makers of Sunlight soap. These industrialists learned from the experiences of the cities in the North of England—the smoke, grime, tightly packed terraced houses, and unsanitary conditions—and they built a new soap manufacturing plant on a large parcel of rural land near the River Mersey. To accommodate their workers, they built attractive, well-equipped houses in blocks, each designed by a different architect, along wide streets, with lots of green space on which children could play. They built schools and a hospital and a temperance hotel. They believed it was important to foster the arts, science, and education generally, so they built an art gallery, they trained their workers, and they gave scholarships to bright children.

Their vision was that healthy, happy families produced the most productive workers. Their approach would be considered paternalistic today, but it worked, and it helped make their company, a forerunner to today's Unilever, an industrial giant.

Apart from wandering through the village and spending a delightful couple of hours in the art gallery, we enjoyed a visit to the museum, which described the history and the underlying vision of the village and contained a number of exhibits that illustrated what it had been like to live and work there in the 19th century.

Ena and I had finished looking at one exhibit describing the kitchen of a typical house, when two elderly couples came up. I say elderly, although from looking in the mirror these days, I have to say that they were more like older brothers and sisters. In any event, they seemed a jovial group who were out for the day on a bus trip, and they wore the requisite clothing for England in midsummer: warm sweaters and skirts or pants and sports jackets. They noticed a bench in front of the exhibit. One of the men produced a digital camera from his pocket.

"Why don't you sit together on the bench, and I'll take your picture?" he said to his companions in what I quickly recognized as a Lancashire accent. The three of them sat on the bench, the ladies taking a moment to fuss with their hair, and they posed for the picture that would shortly be taken. Before the man could do that, Ena, who had been watching this interesting scene, said, "Would you like me to take the picture, so you can all be in it?'

"That's very kind of you," said one of the ladies. The man gave Ena the camera and quickly showed her how to operate it, while the others quietly talked amongst themselves about what a nice offer Ena had made and how a group picture would be a lovely memento of their day together.

"She's a good photographer," I said truthfully, but also wanting to enter into the spirit of what was turning out to be a very pleasant random encounter.

The group sat on the bench, with the two women in the middle and the men on either side. They smiled at the camera held by Ena, and we waited for her to take the picture. She put the camera down.

"I can't see you at all," she said.

"That's because your fingers are over the lens, lass," one of the men said quickly but kindly, and he chuckled. Ena checked, but he was just pulling her leg. Then she realized that the camera hadn't been switched on. She set up again, and everyone took up their poses once more. This time I could tell something else wasn't quite right, because she still looked puzzled. "Is this what I press?" she asked. The man came up and showed her, good naturedly. At last all seemed ready, and the four settled down again. I could see Ena had become a bit flustered by the false starts, but I didn't think anything of it. I held my breath, waiting to hear the quiet click of the shutter. When I heard it, I started to relax, but it was only for a moment.

In a scene unfolding, seemingly in slow motion, before my eyes, I saw the camera fall from Ena's grasp and turn somersaults in mid-air before clattering onto the floor. My heart sank. I thought of the pictures on the camera that might be lost; I thought of the damage to the camera and the cost of repairing or replacing it, but most of all I was sorry for Ena that her act of kindness had ended in this way. All I could say was, "Oh, Ena." I looked over at the group and, much to my amazement, they were laughing their heads off.

"I'm very sorry," Ena blurted out. "It just slipped from my hands," and she bent down to pick up the remains of the camera. To everyone's astonishment, the camera was still in one piece. She examined it and then showed it to the owner. "I think it's not broken after all—it seems to be working. Can you check it?" He gave it a cursory look, still smiling.

"It's just fine," he said. "Please don't worry about it." Now everyone was smiling again. The awkward moment had passed. They were as relieved as we were, partly because the camera wasn't broken, but also, I am sure, because they would not have wanted this accident to happen to anyone. We looked at the picture. Fortunately, it had turned out well, and they were pleased with it. They started giggling amongst themselves as they reflected again on the funny side of what had happened.

"It's just like being on *Candid Camera*," I said, and they laughed again. And it was, except this was for real. Or should I say *reel*? We saw the group several times later on in the day as we were walking. When they saw us, they would nudge each other and begin giggling again. The last time we saw them, the owner of the camera sidled up to Ena.

"We've never laughed so much in a long time. You've made our day," he said as he chuckled. "Yes, by gum. We enjoyed it so much," he said, now laughing loudly. "Can you take another picture of us?"

RESOURCES

- For information on Rotary International and The Rotary Foundation, go to www.rotary.org.
- For information on the Mississauga Lakeshore Rotary Club, go to www.rotarylakeshore.org.
- For information on the child care development centres in South Africa, go to www.soulofafricacharity.org.
- For more background information about this book and the author, please visit www.cuckoosnest.co.